HELP! MY HUSBAND JUST RETIRED

Gwen C. Rollings

Illustrator: Brittany Rollings

Help! My Husband Just Retired
by Gwen C. Rollings

Printed in the United States of America

ISBN 9781622302277

www.xulonpress.com

Dedication

❧ ⑥ ❧

All the women who still believe they will see glorious
sunsets on exotic beaches
And the husbands who promise to walk with them

Acknowledgements

❧ⓖ❧

*M*ore than ten years ago a lady who epitomized all
the qualities I hoped to possess as a senior lady,
Garrison Card, said to me, "You should write a book from a
wife's point of view about retirement." I tucked that thought
away in my mind because my husband was not retired. Last
year I joined a local writers' group. These meetings provide
fertile ground to inspire creativity and the writing process
for published and aspire-to-be authors. For my first assignment, I wrote a story sharing a lesson that I learned about
being "joined at the hip" (a.k.a. too much togetherness)
after my husband retired. Janice Doyle, editor of Senior
Connection, just happened to be there and expressed interest in my doing an article for her magazine. Without her
guidance and encouragement, I might not have written this
book. Then Tim Barrios of Impact Media Creations, to me
a marketing/computer genius, came to one of our writers'
meetings and talked about the possibilities of the Internet

and ebooks. He had the patience of Job as he ran interference for me along this unchartered territory. Finally, my daughter, Brittany, who constantly amazes all who watch as she looks at a blank piece of paper, formulates an idea in her mind, and then instantly produces delightful and amusing characters and drawings. She agreed to do all the illustrations for *Help! My Husband Just Retired*. I look back now and see how God gently took my hand and led me to these people who have meant so much to me and this book. I believe what the Lord promises in Jeremiah 29:11 "I know what I'm doing. I have it all planned out – plans to take care of you, not abandon you, plans to give you the future you hope for."

Golden Years
from Seasons of a Woman

❧ ⑥ ❧

I know what you are thinking
You see my wrinkled brow
And that my hair is graying
My steps are slower now.
You think because you're younger
With youth and energy
That you have the advantage
But I must disagree.
I do not have the hassle
Of hours spent each day
Perfecting my appearance
I feel just fine this way.
And do not think I envy
Your body sleek and trim
While I am watching sunsets

You're sweating at the gym.

You think that I am lonely

Just rocking in my chair

Well, watch out on the dance floor

I'm "two-stepping" out there.

Ah, yes, I love those grandkids

I brag on them with pride

But if they start their crying

Just look for me outside.

You think your mind is sharper

Because I do not do

The things that I don't want to

Who's really fooling who?

Yes, age still has its downside

My parts are wearing out

Because I am a "senior"

I get new ones with discount!

Although you might not yearn for

The pleasures of old age

This sunset of my life is

The brightest of my days.

FOREWARD

☙ ⑥ ❧

I loved every page of Gwen Rollings' book. She made me laugh as she experienced life as the naive wife of a retiree, because I could relate to similarities in my own life and marriage. Gwen humorously describes the challenges she encountered after her husband, Wayne, a Marine Major General, retired and turned the family decision making over to her. The fun comes when he decides <u>how</u> he will go along with her decisions.

Volunteering, grandparent responsibilities, finances, friendships, downsizing possessions, personal space – everything is up for grabs in their retirement! And problems for Gwen aren't necessarily problems to Wayne, who is prone to patiently listening to her dilemma and then deflating the drama by saying, "No one is shooting at you, are they?"

I read the book from beginning to end and was never seriously tempted to put it down. It's a delightful look at the realities of life, marriage, and retirement. It wasn't just the humor that kept me reading. Gwen's use of literary quotes and Biblical passages enlightened each chapter often causing me to pause and contemplate my own expectations at this point of my life's journey.

This story will resonate with most wives in this season of their marriages because it's about a universal paradox: being married and thinking you know everything about that man you love and finding out you don't.

I recommend that you read **Help! My Husband Just Retired** and capture some of Gwen Rollings' zest of life and take to heart her retirement advice to ensure for yourself that the best is yet to come.

Janice Doyle, Editor
Senior Connection Magazine

CONTENTS

ᎧᎧ 6 ᎧᎧ

INTRODUCTION

❧ ⑥ ❧

*R*etirement and giving birth have a lot in common. A husband and wife **talk** about the blessed event. There is **anticipation** that sometime in the future there will be the creation of something which will profoundly affect both of their lives. **Expectations** and **imaginations** of what this new life will be like elicit **excitement** and **apprehension**. **Planning** for this new life is essential for optimum success. There will probably be various degrees of **pain** involved, and **tolerance** to the discomfort in varying degrees is dependent upon the individuals involved. Finally, you never know if there will be **complications** or if the procedure will go smoothly until you actually go through bringing this new life into your world.

Regardless of all the planning and imaginations my husband and I had prior to retirement, we discovered we were surprisingly unprepared for what actually happened. I had this delusion that we would have coffee on the veranda overlooking an ocean view every morning. We would spend blissful days together walking hand-in-hand on deserted beaches, exploring new islands as we travelled to places I'd always wanted to visit. Those were the adventures I assumed would happen for us as a retired couple because of everything I had heard and seen in the retirement brochures, senior citizen magazines' advertisements, and in my retirement dreams.

It's too bad there wasn't a senior citizen retirement reality show that I could have watched on television. At least the propaganda between what is real and what is hype would have been more balanced. Decades of living together never prepared me for what happened when my husband and I were together all the time. That amounts to 168 hours a week and 672 hours a month. After I would say about 2,000 hours of togetherness, I was thinking that I didn't know this man who had been my husband for almost forty years at all! I was not the lone ranger. Almost every other recently retired wife I spoke with wanted to form a support group with me and call it: **HAHA H**usband **A**lways **H**ome **A**nonymous.

For whatever reason, I never questioned another retired wife prior to embarking on this journey. Maybe Medicare should pay for a Senior Wife Mentor to be assigned to every wife when her husband retires. Her sage wisdom could have helped me avoid falling headlong into the numerous expectation pitfalls I didn't see coming. My husband and I attended retirement seminars where practical issues such as finances and medical benefits were discussed, but there was never a presentation by a Senior Wife Mentor entitled "Ladies, life as you knew it is over."

Just as you will never know exactly what that new baby will look or act like until you hold her in your arms, the retirement experience will be unique for every couple. There are times when thinking about our early trials and many errors causes me to laugh until I can hardly catch my breath, and other times when I candidly admit that I could have handled the struggles, minor irritations, and unrealistic expectations I encountered with more patience and love.

If I were given the opportunity for a do-over on some of my illogical retirement decisions, I know this time my new life would be much less traumatic and much more relaxing. That's why I want to give other wives' a heads-up and the real scoop on what to expect as a newly retired wife.

Of course, praying to God and reading the Bible are the never failing-methods of asking for wisdom. The Bible tells us, "Take good counsel and accept corrections – that's the way to live wisely and well." Proverbs 19:20. That is why, after speaking with many other wives whose husbands had retired, I decided that someone needed to write about the good, bad, and just plain crazy experiences wives will probably encounter once they enter the retirement freeway. With the encouragement from these wives, I am casting my ego aside and going out on a limb by revealing what my husband, Wayne, and I encountered through the first years as a retired couple.

I haven't asked my husband if he would agree with me on every aspect of my side of the story. He would probably see our retirement *adventure* a little differently than I did because we normally look at things from a different perspective: men are from Mars. He can write his own book for retired husbands if he wants.

"The road of life twists and turns and no two directions are ever the same. Yet our lessons come from the journey, not the destination." Don Williams, Jr.

THE PROMISE

❧ ⑥ ❧

*I*t has been six years since my husband and I plunged headlong into the uncharted waters of retirement. For over thirty-five years, we were on board the ship of Everyday Life sailing on familiar, though sometimes choppy, seas with other working class Baby Boomers. Then the ship set its final course toward our destinations. Each passenger chose to disembark at a different Port of Call. Some of the passengers had identified their departure location for many years and knew exactly when to get off. Then there were passengers like my husband and me. We were still enjoying the cruise when all of a sudden the ship docked!

This nautical imagery was second nature to me, as was adapting to new surroundings, because I had spent the last thirty-five years as a Department of the Navy, Marine Corps officer's wife. Our family moved over twenty-five times, wherever and whenever the Marine Corps directed. I put my preferences aside, packed up our worldly possession (a.k.a. household goods), the children, and pets, and followed my husband from Camp Lejeune, North Carolina, to Okinawa, Japan, and numerous duty stations in between. I was excited to enter into this *settled* season of our lives.

I thought this lifestyle change would be an intriguing opportunity to play with a brand new deck of cards. All previous bets were off, and I was ready to lay all my cards on an unfamiliar bridge table. This grand finale of my life was going to be the icing on the cake, the pot of gold at the end of the rainbow, the birthday wish finally coming true after blowing out well over half a century's worth of candles… about 2,145 candles should get me something. Like a five year old waking up on her birthday morning, I couldn't wait for the party to begin!

This was the perfect time to remind my husband of The Promise he made to me through the frequent moves and nomadic years: "Honey, whenever I retire from the Marine Corps, you can pick the place to live, and we'll do all the things we never had time to do before." I was chomping at the bit to take on that challenge and orchestrate how *life was supposed to be*. After all, retirement would be a piece of *cake* after thirty-five years in the Marine Corps. I would learn to eat those words. "What to believe and not believe about your husband's retirement promises" should be the first required seminar for all wives.

During the last six years, I have often wished another more experienced retired wife had taken pity on me and become my Senior Wife Mentor. Realizing I was a novice, naïve, and delusional retired wife, she could have kindly and compassionately shared her wisdom by confiding, "Honey, if you ever want to go shopping alone again, you should follow my advice and. . ." Or "Sweetie, you better think twice about doing this before your husband has a chance to. . ." So, I am going to do unto others as I wished someone had done for me. Because forewarned is forearmed, learn from someone who has been there and done that. . . the good, the bad, and the just plain crazy.

WORDS OF WISDOM: "So where does Wisdom come from? And where does Insight live? It can't be found by looking, no matter how deep you dig, no matter how high you fly. If you search through the graveyard and question the dead, they say, 'We've only heard rumors of it.' God alone knows the way to Wisdom, he knows the exact place to find it. He knows where everything is on earth, he sees everything under heaven." Job 28: 20-23

****

"There is a magic in that little world, home; it is a mystic circle that surrounds comforts and virtues never known beyond its hallowed limits." Robert Southey

LOCATION – LOCATION- LOCATION

ᴆ⑥ᴆ

*L*et me start with the just plain crazy. Married to a Major General in the United States Marine Corps, what was I doing sitting alone on a Greyhound Bus? This time I was the one on a mission. My husband stood across the street as the bus pulled onto the highway. His eyes did not leave my face as he crossed his arms against his chest. I waved good-bye with a grin from ear to ear as he continued shaking his head in disbelief until he was completely out of my sight. I settled back in my window seat and prepared for the twenty-nine hour trip ahead.

I smiled remembering how a Greyhound bus forty years ago almost to the day had carried me on another journey that forever changed the course of my life. A high school senior then, I traveled from Massachusetts to South Carolina to attend my brother's graduation from Marine Corps Boot Camp. It was there I met the drill instructor who was to become my husband and the father to our four children. I expected this Greyhound Bus to lead me to another beginning. I was determined that all my expectations for the golden days of retirement were going to come true.

My first goal: location, location, location. Since we had lived all over the world, it was almost overwhelming trying to select one place to put down roots. For over a year I researched areas from Hawaii to Florida. I bought every magazine I could find with articles about the best and worst places to retire. The Internet became my personal real estate agent. Whenever I saw a home in a location that seemed a possibility, I made arrangements to check it out. Depending on the distance, sometimes I drove, several times I took a plane, and I even took a train. I was relentless in my determination to find the perfect house. Then one day, there it was! I found it on the Internet. It was located in rural, northeastern Tennessee. Attempting unsuccessfully to find an airline that flew from our small local airport in South Texas into the small local Tennessee airport, I remained determined to find some way to get there.

This property was just too awesome to pass up, at least that's the way it looked on the Internet advertisement. "Located on twenty acres, two years old, big wrap- around country porch, and a babbling brook running beneath a bridge leading to a quaint, two-story, five bedroom, three bathroom country home." I told my husband I was sure this place was IT. My husband had other commitments and wasn't able to drive with me. He didn't think it was safe for me to drive by myself that far. That's why I was on a Greyhound bus. I had no choice.

Wayne was not overjoyed when I discussed my plan. "Are you crazy? Do you know how long you'll be riding on a bus to get there? You haven't ridden on a bus for forty years, and you're not as young as you used to be." He saw the reality while I saw the possibilities. My motto: if you can dream it, you can achieve it. I saw the trip as another adventure – the road less travelled.

Twenty-nine hours later, I understood why it was the road less travelled. Although I was not yet ready to admit Wayne was right about my bus decision, I would concede it was challenging to sleep on a bus with a stranger snoring in the seat next to me. Also, crawling over someone to get to the restroom in the middle of the night presented its own unique obstacles. Oh, well, I survived…at least one way.

The driver dropped me off at small bus station in Tennessee. I asked directions from the lone ticket agent to get me to the rental car lot. Pulling my suitcase behind me along the broken sidewalk, I noticed a dilapidated pickup truck slowing down as the ten or more men, women, and children stuffed in the truck's front seat and bed unashamedly gawked at me. I guess I looked like a well-to-do homeless person at that point. The tobacco chewing driver raised his arm dangling down from the open window and said, "Howdy." Uncomfortable with their stares, I wondered how they would look after a twenty nine hour bus trip. . . well, probably not much different.

The mountains were breathtaking. The air was crisp, fresh, and clean. Walking the few blocks to obtain my rental car, I became rejuvenated and excited about meeting with the realtor who was to take me to view the house. I arrived in the town a few hours before our appointment, and I couldn't stand the suspense of waiting. I went into the small post office and asked how I could find the address so I could take a peek before the realtor gave me a tour.

The postman replied, "Up there's where they make the moonshine."

"Moonshine, what do you mean?"

"Oh, they still make whiskey up there," he replied, laughing.

Surely, he must be joking I assured myself as I walked out with his written directions to the house. He wasn't. After driving out of town on a paved highway, I veered off onto an isolated dirt road for about five miles which reminded me of scenes from the movie *Deliverance*. In a clearing sat the house from the Internet picture though it did not have the same effect in living color. Oh, there were twenty acres, which went straight up a mountain that began ten feet from the back porch. Blue paint was peeling all over the wrap-around porch and wood siding like strings of spaghetti, not detectable in the pristine Internet photo. The brook running in the front yard was not so much babbling as clanking from all the bottles and cans floating downstream. Obviously, this was not to be my dream house.

I called the realtor from my cell phone when I finally had reception, cancelled the showing, drove as fast as I could back to civilization, spent the night in a local hotel, got back on the bus, rode for another twenty-nine hours, having learned a valuable lesson. A more appropriate definition of *personal freedom* is never being completely certain you're making the right choice! At least in the Marine Corps, we always knew where we were going next. We didn't have a set of orders now directing us to our duty station, and I didn't know where to go. All my exhausting attempts to find the perfect location were like finding that proverbial needle in a haystack. I might as well pick a home by throwing a dart at a map of the United States for all the luck I was having. I thought selecting a permanent home for us after thirty-five years of a nomadic lifestyle would be a walk in the park, not a marathon bus ride!

Somewhere along the way back to Texas, I realized that a few, well most, of my predetermined, foregone conclusions about life were a bit unrealistic anyway, like I would be one of those rare women who actually looked younger with gray hair. I expected retirement to be *the best is yet to come* automatically arriving. I was acting like a five year old waking up on my birthday morning, planning every detail of my own surprise party, and then being surprised because it didn't turn out the way I'd planned.

Wayne met me at the same bus stop where I had left 58-plus hours before. This time he was smiling, and I was shaking my head in disbelief. How could he have let me get on that bus in the first place? The trip wasn't all bad. Someone I met on the bus gave me some good advice. She suggested I should rent a house for a few months in the area before I jumped in with both feet and bought a home. I remember she was a retired wife, too, and had been there and done that. That is actually excellent advice because home ownership is not all it's cracked up to be in retirement. I wanted fewer responsibilities - not more. We didn't take her advice.

Words of Wisdom: God knows what he is doing. He has it all planned out. He has plans to take care of you, not abandon you, plans to give you the future you hope for. Jeremiah 29: 11

****

"A compromise is the art of dividing a cake in such a way that everyone believes he has the biggest piece."

Ludwig Erhard

COMPROMISE WHENEVER POSSIBLE

❦⑥❦

*A*fter much prayer and seeking God's direction this time, at least we narrowed our search to the Southeast United States. I could see myself sitting under a palm tree, gentle breezes blowing through my hair as I watched seagulls flying in the sun. Like a Jimmy Buffet song, I wanted to be able to watch a glorious sunset every night, go where the weather suited my clothes, sailing on a summer breeze. Well, you get the tropical picture here. However, I neglected to consider one small piece of my coconut pie dream: my husband and where he wanted to live.

When Wayne said I could pick the place, I thought he meant *I could pick the place*. He somehow forgot to mention that I could pick the place as long as he agreed with me.

If I had attended that first wives' seminar, **What to believe and not believe about your husband's retirement promises**, I might have anticipated this slight deflection in his promise. He did not envision himself sitting under that palm tree with me, because he argued it would get hot wearing his preferred attire of jeans and cowboy boots. In fact, he told me, "If you ever find me wearing some Hawaiian print shorts, and socks with sandals, you better know I've lost my mind. So put me in an old soldiers' home."

When asked for his input, Wayne disclosed his preference for a retirement location: someplace like Mayberry, RFD (remember Andy Taylor and Aunt Bee?) He was obviously remembering his childhood days in rural South Carolina. I never lived in the country and never wanted to live where there wasn't a shopping mall within 15 minutes. I don't like to cook, much less put stuff up in glass jars. Chickens or any farm animals would mean a lot of work and never getting to go anyplace because they can't feed or milk themselves. Oh, no, I would not "pick" somewhere like Mayberry for the rest of my life.

I knew we would have to reach some kind of meeting of the minds. I could have taken a stand, drawn a line in the sand (under that palm tree), and insisted my husband make good on his promise to let me choose; however, I had lived long enough to know that forcing anyone to do anything is like making your ten-year- old son eat broccoli before he can leave the table. He may put the broccoli in his mouth, but he will spit it out as soon as the coast is clear.

So I got a pencil and paper, and the two of us listed the five most important factors about where we wanted to live. We finally came up with a workable game plan. My husband said I could choose anywhere I wanted, but he preferred it to be below the Mason-Dixon Line, and he didn't want to live right next door to someone else's house. He had been raised in the country, so he wanted a few acres to "spread out."

Spread out, what did that mean? We had been living on top of our next door neighbors on Marine bases for over thirty years. Now, I discovered he wanted "land, lots of land, under sunny skies above." Although I needed nothing more than a small condo near some great beach to make me happy, I magnanimously acknowledged that I wanted both of us to be satisfied, and I would be willing to compromise again. I was confident I would find the perfect spot to suit us both because there would be a rainbow over it. Actually, I believed in my heart that God would lead me, and I would see the promised land and say, "This is it."

Florida seemed to be the state that satisfied the most points on each of our lists. We both wanted someplace warm and near water. Having come to an agreement on the state, we only had to narrow our final decision down to the exact location for us in Florida. I was breathing a sigh of relief, because we were only talking one little state, right? The only hesitation was: we never lived in Florida before. I convinced myself that so many retired people move to Florida, there must be plenty of good reasons for thousands of retirees making this choice. I was trying hard to hear that still small voice telling me I was on the right track. I hadn't heard it yet. As I've gotten older, I discovered that listening to my gut feeling is always a wise decision. I would advise all wives to wait until there is a peace about a decision before making it.

WORDS OF WISDOM: "Trust God from the bottom of your heart: don't try to figure out everything on your own. Listen for God's voice in everything you do, everywhere you go; he's the one who will keep you on track. Don't assume that you know it all."

Proverbs 3: 5 - 6

****

"Retirement, we understand, is great if you are busy, rich and healthy. But then, under those circumstances, work is great too." William E Bill Vaughan

PICKLE BALL

꙰ ⑥ ꙰

*P*ickle ball. If you've been to a 55 plus community, you know about pickle ball. When Wayne and I were debating our move to Florida, we visited several playgrounds for seniors. One of our friends called them places where people were on a perpetual twenty-four hour recess. The advertisements in magazines and even on the television substantiated his claim. The ads depicted tanned, athletic, gray-haired, always smiling men and women who were riding bicycles, dancing in the town square, playing golf, and engaging in a team sport called pickle ball. It looked like a playground where I wanted to spend my recess. Before we made our final decision about where to live, we sent an email to one of the largest senior planned communities in Florida asking for information. It was advertised as the Disney World for Retirees.

The well-organized marketing department planned a whole day for us to preview the facilities. The realtor assigned to us, Frank, looked like a poster boy for seniors. He was tall, tanned, and attractive. He was introduced to us by a smiling, uniformed Visitor's Greeter at the lavishly decorated Information Center. Leather club chairs grouped in intimate settings on hardwood floors, and fireplaces in tastefully decorated, library-like rooms brought familiar glimpses reminiscent of back home to all the northerners considering relocation. Refreshments reflected Southern Hospitality at its finest. I decided I would like to live in the Information Center.

Frank put us in the back seat of a snazzy golf cart, and the whirlwind tour began. That's when I witnessed pickle ball. It's like a slow motion version of tennis using a white, light-weight plastic ball instead of a tennis ball. There was some fierce competition going on among those seniors, and it seemed to be a great workout as they kept bending over to pick up the missed balls from the court.

If pickle ball was not your forte, no need to stay home and become a recluse. We were told that over 1,000 activities are available for residents. Although not possible to see every-thing in a day, Frank knew how to tease us. We saw just one of the many swimming pools where, coincidentally, there was a synchronized swimming class in session. I never saw that many bathing caps at one time in a pool moving about in such slow, but fully in sync, motion. As the class finished, and all the swimmers passed us going to the locker room, I thought, "Hey, I would never have to feel self conscious again about how I looked if I lived here. I could go out in a bathing suit and fit right in."

Then Frank drove us by cheerleading practice. I was a cheerleader in high school, and those were great times. These women in their T-shirts and short skirts were obviously having a great time, too. With their pom-poms and headbands, they practiced a cheer...in slow motion. I was encouraged to see women older than I not wearing long, flowered dresses, with their hair in buns, sitting in a rocking chair. No one was wearing your mother's jeans here.

I never experienced anything like this amusement park for seniors' environment, but I could tell Wayne was thinking people would not be acting this way in Mayberry. Retirement used to mean people could quit the factory job or their normal place of business and finally take life easy. The new message celebrated fitness, fun, and frivolity at a frenzied pace. This philosophy was validated by the 486 holes of golf and the 9,000 tee times per day, the fitness centers, hula lessons, golf cart drill teams, sports, bands, vocal groups, craft centers, theatre, dancing nightly on the town square, and concerts with big name entertainers weekly.

Finally, Frank showed us some of the housing areas that fit into what we wanted and could afford. There was an area for every socioeconomic retirement pay: well designed and neat mobile home parks, condos, townhouses, duplexes, single family homes, and mansions. Each neighborhood seemed to have its own unique personality with special activities and clubs for just those residents. We heard the neighbors often got together at each other's homes for barbeques, parties, and holidays. The marketing brochures Frank provided to us promised we would discover the friendliest neighborhoods in Florida. The instant acceptance into the community clubs, organizations, and social events began to sound familiar and comfortable to me almost like the environment I knew and loved around the military housing areas.

Riding through the different areas, I held on to Wayne's arm as other golf cart drivers in their 70's, 80's, and older zoomed around us like they were on the Indianapolis Speedway. Their driving was the only activity I witnessed not in slow motion. There were no children around any of the neighborhoods. Frank told us that children are welcome but only for no more than three weeks at a time. Then they are out of there. He said residents were happy never to have to deal with the noise, school buses, and all the other annoyances that children bring to life. He proudly called the areas "age appropriate."

Frank, a senior himself, seemed as tuckered out as Wayne and I were. He was paid to get us committed to buying a home and becoming one of the 90,000 residents in this senior wonderland. Deciding to end our search here for our retirement location was so tempting to me because of all the fun activities and people I could get to know. I was already picturing myself with pom-poms and wearing that cute cheerleader outfit.

I had only one hesitation: I loved to be around children, watch them ride their bikes through the neighborhood, and knock on our door for trick-or-treat on Halloween. They keep me young, they nourish my soul, and they make me laugh. I admit to being a 55-plus, senior citizen, oldie, golden girl, whatever term people delegate for those of us who have lived long enough to rate a senior discount, but my heart still feels young, and children keep a song in it. No, not ready for the pom-poms yet. Wayne gave a sigh of relief as we drove away from the senior wonderland as I looked at him and said, "No, I don't pick this place."

WORDS OF WISDOM: "I looked long and hard at what goes on around here, and let me tell you, things are bad. And people feel it. There are people, for instance, on whom God showers everything – money, property, reputation – all they ever wanted or dreamed of. And then God doesn't let them enjoy it. Some stranger comes along and has all the fun. It's more of what I'm calling *smoke*. A Bad business. Say a couple have scores of children and live a long, long life but never enjoy themselves – even though they end up with a big funeral!. . . Even if someone lived a thousand years – make it two thousand! – but didn't enjoy anything, what's the point? Doesn't everyone end up in the same place? We work to feed our appetites; meanwhile our souls go hungry."

Ecclesiastes 6: 1 - 7

"Many times I wondered if I were truly carrying out God's plan for my life."

Lawrence Welk

HOME AT LAST

ཀྵ ⑥ ཀྵ

*W*ayne was a highly decorated Marine for his efforts in Viet Nam with the elite Force Reconnaissance Company. He was calm and composed about most situations that I proclaimed to be crises. He normally remarked, "No one is shooting at you, so what's the problem?" He obviously had a lot of nerve. He returned to Texas to finish up his job there and left *me* in Florida to *pick the place.* Did he remember I was the one who rode on a Greyhound bus for fifty-eight hours? Maybe someone shooting at him would have been safer than me picking out a house.

It takes a lifetime of living together for a husband to finally recognize that his wife has contributed to and sometimes made by herself most of the major decisions in their lives anyway and had his back, as the saying goes, through good times and bad.

If trust is not a major component of the marriage at the retirement stage, the journey will not be pleasant moving forward.

Wisely this time, I resisted the temptation to make this decision without asking for help. I needed guidance not only about the house we would buy but also about fitting into God's plan for our lives from this point on. Like most couples our age, working and raising a family had consumed our thoughts and energies for the last thirty or forty years. There was a measure of anticipation yet discomfort in the unknown elements of such a drastic life change. We were confident of one thing: we wanted to leave nothing on the table of our lives when the feast was over. Where we lived, what we did, and who we met along this stretch of the journey would punctuate and define a life well lived.

Knowing whatever retirement location we chose would significantly influence our future, I prayed for God's leadership in guiding *us* to the home He had selected. I also asked for Him to give us a peace when in the process of making the right decision. He did both. The realtor showed me several beautiful properties. Each would fit our needs. I was ready to make an offer on a lovely home in a gated community but didn't feel the inner peace I had asked God to provide. I asked the realtor to check if there were any other properties on the market I could see before making my final decision. She looked on her Multiple Listing Service and made an appointment to view only one more.

The realtor and I drove to the six-acre horse farm, complete with four horse stalls, swimming pool, three paddocks, and hundred-year-old granddaddy oaks festooned with Spanish moss. I immediately felt like I was coming home. The Home Owners' Association Covenants sealed the deal for me. The Covenants section on **Restrictions** said in bold print that all farm animals (chickens, pigs, cows, etc.) were prohibited and only horses were allowed there. This was perfect. It was only fifteen minutes from the shopping mall and had six acres of land for Wayne to spread out on. I was certain I saw a rainbow hovering over the fields.

I called Wayne, and he said to make an offer on the property. We prayed if it was God's will, that the offer would be accepted without any further negotiations. It was accepted. So we turned the page to this new chapter titled *Retirement*. Packing our worldly treasures (a.k.a. household goods) one more time, we moved from Texas to our retirement home in Ocala, Florida. God is good. So we marked off the *location* block on our list of retirement prerequisites and began to settle in as new retirees.

The realtors assured us that Ocala was in the most secure spot in the state and that hurricanes rarely came close to this beautiful countryside with rolling hills and few palm trees. It was easy to believe because the closest beach was a couple of hours away on either side of us. The year we moved to Florida, I lost confidence in those realtors' predictions. Three hurricanes hit in rapid succession, crossing the middle of the state and hitting Ocala hard. We lost water and electricity temporarily, and several of the oldest granddaddy oaks forever.

One morning after the final hurricane barreled through Ocala, there was no doubt in my mind that I had made the wrong decision in moving there. I had just stepped out of bed when I saw it. I must be mistaken, I thought. I stood very still, but it did not. Slithering across the rug in the bedroom was about a twelve-inch long black snake. It could have been a thirty-foot python as far as I was concerned – a snake is a snake. No one was in the house but me. I was not about to wait for someone to return while the snake took up secret residence in our new home.

I calmly went to the kitchen, brought a broom back to the bedroom, and swept the unwelcome visitor out through the patio door and down the steps. For whatever reason, he (or she) never offered any resistance and politely slipped off into the woods. It was just a test. We had prayed about moving to this place, and like Moses in the Wilderness, we would just shake off snakes or any other doubts that might creep in taking away our trust in Him who led us here.

However, the thought also crossed my mind that maybe God arranged for me to meet that lady on the bus who suggested we just rent a house first. Moses was ready at a moment's notice to move his tent to another place if God said so. He didn't have to contact a realtor and try to sell his tent in a bad economy before he could relocate. I would advise another wife at this rent/buy junction in the retirement road to consider the pro's and con's. If another snake found its way into my bedroom, I was prepared to pull up my stakes and move my tent fast.

WORDS OF WISDOM: God says, "I will always show you where to go. I'll give you a full life in the emptiest of places – firm muscles, strong bones. You'll be like a well-watered garden, a gurgling spring that never runs dry. You'll use the old rubble of past lives to build anew, rebuild the foundations from out of your past. You'll be known as those who can fix anything, restore old ruins, rebuild and renovate, make the community livable again." Isaiah 58: 10 - 12

****

"But let there be spaces in your togetherness and let the winds of the heavens dance between you. Love one another but make not a bond of love: let it be a moving sea between the shores of your souls." Kahlil Gibran

ME AND MY SHADOW, STROLLING DOWN THE AVENUE

❧ ⑥ ❧

*T*he neighborhood wives asked me over for coffee shortly after we moved into our retirement home. When I shared with these seasoned retired wives my excitement about finally being able to spend quality time with my husband, a glaze seemed to cover their eyes, and they fell silent. Their reactions were perplexing to me. I hoped they could give me some encouragement, but I received nothing. Like someone reporting on her afterlife experience, a wife of a dearly retired working *soul* could have guided me in maneuvering the many twists and turns on the journey ahead. Although I would not equate retirement with heaven (or hell), I met people who were convinced retirement was like one place or the other. I needed an advice angel!

If another wife should ask me how I would describe my first days of retirement, I would be honest, frank, and pull no punches. I would use a medical analogy. Retirement seemed to me like coming out of a coma. I remembered aspects of my life before the head trauma, but things just seem out of place. Pre-retirement, my husband and I would run errands together on the weekend. Post-retirement, every day seemed like a Saturday. We had our morning coffee together as we'd done for forty years, but then he didn't leave to go to work… or anywhere…all day…without me. We went everywhere together. We ate out at least once a day, went to the library together, grocery shopping pushing one cart, and attended the same classes at church. We didn't even go to get gas in the car without the other one along. Being joined at the hip was novel, fun, like an extended vacation until that day at the beauty shop.

I had been going to Maxine's to get my hair done every four weeks for several months. She knew more about me than my own mother. We talked about our husbands and children and shared personal things about life. Like sitting next to a stranger on an airplane, the talk was innocent and safe because you knew your separate lives would never converge. One Tuesday that all changed.

My husband drove me to my appointment with Maxine and was dropping off a library book before he came back to get me. Then we were going to his barber for a haircut. Maxine and I had our usual girl talk. She applied the color and left me reading a magazine. After a few minutes I glanced over at the caped client in the next chair. *My* husband smiled back as *my* Maxine clipped away on his hair.

Maxine was laughing and chatting up a storm with my husband. I felt like my cover had been blown. I would have to enter the witness protection program after Maxine turned into a snitch. I mistakenly thought their lives would never converge (like the stranger on the airplane.) I tried hard to read Maxine's lips so I could start planning my counter strategy when I had to explain those cute little stories I had shared about him with Maxine. I tried hard to remember. What had I told her that could get me in hot water?

Although I couldn't hear what they were saying, I was certain I saw Maxine mouth the words, "You should come here more often." That was not going to happen. I would make sure that was my husband's first and last beauty appointment with Maxine. I now understood the glazed looks and silence from those other retired wives when I mentioned spending quality time with my husband. It is possible to have too much of a good thing.

WORDS OF WISDOM: "Don't, by the way, read too much into the differences here between men and women. Neither man nor woman can go it alone or claim priority. Man was created first, as a beautiful shining reflection of God–that is true. But the head on a woman's body clearly outshines in beauty the head of her "head" her husband. The first woman came from man, true-but ever since then, every man comes from a woman! And since virtually everything comes from God anyway, let's quit going through these 'who's first' routines." 1 Corinthians 11:10 – 12

"Never idealize others. They will never live up to your expectations. Don't over-analyze your relationships. Stop playing games. A growing relationship can only be nurtured by genuineness." Leo F. Buscaglia

EXPECTATIONS

❧ ⑥ ❧

I planned it all out. We would take wonderful, exotic vacations as members of the crew on a sailboat in the South Pacific. We would take ballroom dancing lessons at the senior center and become the couple everyone watched on the country club dance floor. In our spare time, we would take a photography course at the community college to prepare us to capture all the wonderful memories we were going to make.

There was only one tiny detail to work out: *my husband.* He wasn't into working as a crew member on a sailboat. Wayne said during his time as a Marine that he had been on enough ships to last a lifetime. He couldn't understand why we needed dancing lessons because I'd never complained about how he danced before. He thought the disposable instamatic cameras from Walgreen's he had used for years took great pictures — all just minor obstacles for me to overcome. Wrong!

To be completely honest, I harbored my secret doubts about the retirement party. After all, I didn't get that bicycle I *really* wanted when I was eight, and not every party turned out to be as much fun as I had envisioned. Every retired wife will eventually come to realize this truism: the best indicator of present and future behavior is past behavior. Even though I proclaimed that "all bets were off" and I was "playing with a different deck of cards," I knew Wayne and I were not receiving lobotomies with our Medicare retirement packages. We retained our basic personalities, our perceptions about what was important to us as individuals, and what we liked or didn't like to do. What did change was the *way* I looked at the actions, behaviors, and hobbies he had maintained throughout our marriage.

A great example to illustrate this mental shift in thinking is golf. I listened to more wives than I can count complain throughout our pre-retirement years about husbands playing golf. "He cares more about golf than he does about his family." "He's out playing golf, and it's been snowing most of the morning." "It's a good thing I went into labor the day the golf course was closed, or I'd have been driving myself to the hospital." "The person who invented golf needs to be locked in the toy room with my five kids all day."

How different days are in the post-retirement years when too much togetherness can force a wife to leave home and drive around absent mindedly even in a golf cart for hours just to get away from the call of the wild, "Honey, where are you?" The conversations from post-retirement wives go something like this: "My husband plays golf on Friday, so I'm free that day. Thank Goodness. I've tried to talk him into playing golf more often." "Honey, that hurricane is not supposed to hit for at least a few hours. You just go out and enjoy yourself on the golf course. It will do you good." "What do you mean your foursome was cancelled? Can't you just go out there and make new friends to play with."

We thought we wanted things different, a new and improved spouse, but maybe not. There are so few things in life that stay the same. Like the familiarity of your husband's special, slightly past-its-prime recliner. Molded by years of supporting him, body and soul, day and night, it fits him just right. You might threaten to replace it, but you can't. Even though the arms are a little frayed, and it might not recline as far back as it did once, it is too comfortable to change.

61

If Wayne had suddenly started wearing a Hawaiian shirt and flip flops, he wouldn't be my Wayne. He might not want to take dancing lessons, but I was comfortable in his arms as we moved at our own rhythm across the floor. I normally forgot to take along even the Walgreen's instamatic camera to capture our celebrations. We captured them where it counts the most—in our hearts and memories.

That's not to say that retirement isn't a great time to do things you've always wanted to do but just never had the time or opportunity to do them. Unfortunately, we discovered that many things seem much more exciting in theory than they are in practice. We decided to buy a pontoon boat. It just seemed natural that living in Florida meant we should own a boat. Although we had never had an inclination to own a large boat before, retirement seemed like the perfect time. Being crew members on a boat would be exciting for two armchair sailors. We were cautioned before our purchase that the two best days in owning a boat are: the day you buy it and the day you sell it. That was true for us. Maybe renting a boat before buying one is good advice, too.

I would advise women looking for ways to add a little excitement to spice up their lives in retirement to start with that old recliner. Perhaps a colorful pillow?

WORDS OF WISDOM: "My dear lover glows with health – red-blooded, radiant! He's one in a million. There's no one quite like him!. . . Everything about him delights me, thrills me through and through! That's my lover, that's my man." Song of Songs 5:10, 16

"All married couples should learn the art of battle as they should learn the art of making love. Good battle is objective and honest –never vicious or cruel. Good battle is healthy and constructive, and brings to a marriage the principle of equal partnership." Ann Landers

THE ART OF BATTLE

∞ 6 ∞

*S*ix months into retirement, I decided there are two honeymoon periods in a marriage: one after the wedding and one after retirement. Becoming man and wife, we embarked on a life that was unfamiliar to Wayne or me. His routines were different than my routines. Cute little quirks I never noticed before, like Wayne taking twenty-three various vitamin pills after dinner every night, and the way he loved to watch his favorite football teams on television, I thought he was just adorable. Every day in the beginning of our marriage I learned something new about him. He was my prince charming.

After five or six months, there suddenly appeared chinks in the Prince's armor. I used the same bathroom, and why were there twenty-three bottles of vitamins all over the counter? I had to put my perfume and stuff there, too. Why did a young man in excellent health have to take all those pills anyway and right after dinner? I was sure he did that so he wouldn't have to help me clean up the dishes.

Sure, Wayne told me to wait and he would help, but he took absolutely too long to come back. He knew I wanted to get the kitchen cleaned so I could sit down and watch my favorite shows. That was another thing, we only had one television set, and I was not about to sit there and watch those boring football games every time one came on. Whenever I was forced to confront him, in a loving way, of course, and share that had I noticed his lack of consideration and thoughtlessness toward me before we were married, things might have taken a different turn. That was the first time Wayne gave me the *'what is she talking about'* look. That honeymoon period was over.

We began assigning roles and responsibilities in order to coordinate a marriage and a life together. I paid the bills and handled all administrative matters such as paying taxes and keeping track of our personal and financial paperwork. Wayne worked and provided well for his family throughout the years. We functioned in sync, like a well-oiled machine, in performing household matters. There were few conflicts because we knew what we were supposed to do.

Fast forward almost forty years to retirement. Becoming a retired man and wife, we embarked on a life that was unfamiliar to Wayne or me. His routines were different than my routines. Cute little quirks, like Wayne's affinity for going to Walmart every day and wanting me to go along, and his offer to clean up the kitchen after dinner every night, I thought were just adorable. Often in the beginning months of retirement, I discovered endearing qualities that I had never noticed about him. He was king of our retirement castle.

After five or six months, the queen was ready to say, "Off with his head." Yes, some Walmart stores stayed open twenty-four hours day, but I didn't enjoy accompanying him at ten o'clock at night because he needed something for the first thing in the morning. Although emptying the dishwasher was considerate of my husband, it was like a game of hide and seek for my utensils whenever I started to cook. How do you, lovingly, tell your husband you don't want to go everyplace with him, to put things back where they belong, and stop rearranging your kitchen?

I didn't.

However, in the functioning together as a well-oiled machine situation, some parts began to malfunction. I always mailed in renewals for our car and license registrations and took care of any administrative matters. That was my job. Now Wayne decided anything with his name on it should be his responsibility. When his driver's license renewal came in the mail several months before it was to expire, I mentioned Wayne should just mail it in. He didn't want to do that. He wanted to go to the DMV office and pick it up. I tried to tell him that was not a good idea.

Almost two months later, a week before his driver's license was due to expire he decided he would go into the local DMV office. Four hours later, he returned. After waiting for the thirty people before him to be processed, his number was called. He was told he needed to bring in his birth certificate. This former Marine was furious because he had taken in his military I.D., and the DMV would not accept that for documentation.

After he had ranted and raved about the time he wasted and nothing getting accomplished. I had to say it. I knew it was wrong, but I had to say, "I told you so." He never learned how to maneuver the *system* of getting through the red tape of renewals. How quickly he mastered that skill would depend on listening to a seasoned veteran (me) of the governmental red tape battles. We will always have differences of opinion because someone once told me after my first honeymoon period was over, "If you and your husband never have any conflicts or arguments, one of you is unnecessary."

Retirement was an opportunity for us to start a Honeymoon II chapter in the same book we had been writing together for so many years. Seasoned verbal debaters, this time we anticipated familiar quirks were not going to suddenly disappear. Although we attempted to negotiate the conflicts as best we could, that's not to say it was always smooth sailing. Retirement created different boundary lines for each of us. When Wayne trespassed over my lines, I didn't like it. He probably felt the same when I stepped over his need for privacy, but he never got upset. "No one was shooting at him."

Many wives think there is nothing they don't know about their husbands after living with them for decades. The dynamics of retirement means you might be playing with the same deck of cards, but the rules have changed about how to play the game. I negotiated my own set of rules. I don't go anyplace that I really don't want to go unless it is extremely important to Wayne. He insists on cleaning up the kitchen if I cook and unloading the dishwasher from time to time which was never the way we played this game of marriage before. I always say, "Thank you, Honey." Life is too short to sweat the small stuff, and honeymoons can't last forever.

WORDS OF WISDOM: "Where do you think all these appalling wars and quarrels come from? Do you think they just happen? Think Again. They come about because you want your own way, and fight for it deep inside yourselves. You lust for what you don't have and are willing to kill to get it. You want what isn't yours and will risk violence to get your hands on it. You wouldn't think of just asking God for it, would you?" James 4: 1 - 2

****

"I'm not saying my wife's a bad cook, but she uses a smoke alarm as a timer."

Bob Monkhouse

COOKIES AND CONVERSATION

∞⑥∞

"*My* house is dark, and my pots are cold" was a verse in a popular song from my era. Although I didn't get the intended message back then, I was certain now those words were written for many retired wives, especially me. I would be happy to never cook again. Hamburger Helper, Tuna Helper, Chicken Helper...I needed all the helpers I could get in the kitchen. For forty years I was the chief cook and bottle washer in our family, but I had never asked for the job.

I should have done a prenup. The only stipulation I would have put in a prenuptial agreement: *The parties to the aforementioned marriage agree the wife will not assume any duties remotely associated or simulated to resemble cooking.* I said "I do," but I could not say "I don't" to kitchen duty. What made this situation even worse, it seemed to me that every other wife and mother on the planet in the 60's *loved* to cook.

I was introduced to The Bake Sale when my oldest daughter entered kindergarten. All the parents were asked to bring in baked goods. I mentioned to another mother that I would probably buy some cookies at the grocery store. She looked at me as if I had said, "I never intend to go over my daughter's spelling words with her before the Friday tests."

I got the message and brought in my version of chocolate chip cookies. Even though they were thin and crunchy, without that perfectly round (boring) shape people had come to expect, and even though it was for a good cause, not one sold. For the remaining school years, I realized that nothing says loving like something from someone else's oven. The local bakery's cookies were always the first to go at the bake sales. I did improve through the years, mostly through trial and error, but I wasn't sorry when the bake sale phase of life ended for me.

As we became acquainted with more retired couples, we began receiving invitations to their homes for dinner. Wayne couldn't understand why I kept making excuses not to accept them. He finally asked, "Hey, you keep saying you want to make friends, but when they ask us over you make excuses not to go. You know it doesn't matter to me if it's just the two of us, but don't complain about not having friends then."

"I do want to have friends, but why do we have to go to their houses for dinner?" I reasoned. "Couldn't we just meet them at Perkins or Bob Evans like all the other retirees? You know what always happens next after we go to their homes for dinner?" Certain he would know what happened next I waited for him to respond. Instead he gave me one of those "I have no idea what you're talking about" expressions that, by the way, was really getting on my nerves. "Oh, come on. Then we'll have to invite them to our house for dinner, and the *who's the best cook* contest begins again."

Wayne had been through enough dinner parties with me to know cooking was not one of my spiritual gifts. He suggested we accept a couple of dinner invitations and when it was our turn to reciprocate, he would grill out to make it easy on me. A barbeque would be a great idea. Then it would become a man thing. Men can become very competitive when you give them a bag of charcoal and a match. Let him feel my pain for once.

We went to several homes for dinner, and I was pleasantly surprised. Most people in our age group were more concerned with healthy and affordable meals than with impressing us with their culinary expertise. Chicken, normally the main course, was cooked in some type of low calorie sauce concoction with rice and a steamed vegetable. Sometimes we were served a side salad and fruit for dessert. Yes, I could do that!

Except when it was our turn to have people over, Wayne insisted he was going to keep his part of the bargain. His barbeque chicken, grilled veggies, and baked potatoes received raves from our dinner guests. At last one of my dessert recipes, Pink Surprise, was actually requested every time I made it. I took a small can of crushed pineapple, a small sweetened condensed milk, a can of cherry pie filling, a large carton of non-dairy whipped topping, mixed all the ingredients together in a glass bowl and froze it before the dinner party. Simple abundance!

I knew if there was a senior bake sale benefiting a good cause now that people would probably buy my own home baked cookies. Even if my cookies were rejected, I would remind myself that I never remember the sweet cakes and cookies I bought at a bake sale, but I always remember the sweet bakers who made me feel accepted.

I realized something even more significant through these dinners that I should have learned years ago. The spiritual gift of hospitality is not meant to impress people with your cooking ability. It is your welcoming ability. It is the comfortable conversations, sharing about families, connecting with another person at more than a superficial level but at a heart level. I've heard it said that you never really know another person until you break bread together. Thank goodness for great bakeries.

WORDS OF WISDOM: "Then he (Jesus) turned to the host. "The next time you put on a dinner, don't just invite your friends and family and rich neighbors, the kind of people who will return the favor. Invite some people who never get invited out, the misfits from the wrong side of the tracks. You'll be – and experience – a blessing. They won't be able to return the favor, but the favor will be returned – oh, how it will be returned! – at the resurrection of God's people." Luke 14: 12 - 14

****

"Industry, thrift, and self control are not sought because they create wealth, but because they create character."

Calvin Cooledge

SUPER COUPONING

e were coupon-challenged novices at the beginning. My husband and I enjoyed eating out several times during weekends until he retired. Now that every day seemed like Saturday, we began eating out almost every day. Our first few months' bill for eating out totaled almost more than our mortgage payments. Then we learned the system

Vanity will never get senior discounts. I remember being offended the first time I was charged for a senior coffee at a fast food restaurant. That cashier, who looked twelve years old, never even asked if I was old enough to receive a senior discount. I saw it on the bill "Senior coffee $.40." After the initial shock wore off, I decided senior discounts were a good thing, and I should just get over thinking 60 is the new 40.

Although I was never thrilled when others, especially those X Generation youngsters, referred to us as senior citizens, I realized getting substantial discounts just for living so long mitigated my agitation a little. I obviously looked old enough for discounts, and I needed to face that senior fact or better said: fact that senior face!

The Internet was like a discount Pandora's Box. I discovered that 921 restaurants near our metropolitan area offered some sort of senior discounts. So what if we had to make a few minor adjustments to our daily schedules and egos. Flexibility must be a factor in the restaurant discount game. We've always heard that the early bird catches the worm. Well, the early bird special included two eggs (any way), two strips of bacon, two slices of toast, and a cup of coffee for $2.99. You had to be there at 6:00 a.m. to get a seat to beat out all the other old birds. That senior dinner special meant you'd be eating again at 2:00 p.m., but you'd be ready at that time because you ate breakfast at 6:00 a.m.

Like everything with these reduced meal prices, there were some concessions. The fifty-five plus baked chicken dinner at one popular chain restaurant included a breast the size of a sparrow's and two stems of broccoli – no rolls. The amount of food could be compared to a kid's meal because of the petite portions. Actually, they should have included a senior toy to make it at least as equitable for us old kids, too.

So what if I had to spend a little time researching and locating the restaurants offering the best deals, it was worth the savings. One time I selected a restaurant with $$$$ (on a scale of $ to $$$$) on the Internet site because it offered a large percentage for senior discount on the meal. I figured $$$$ with discount would probably be equal to $$. We could handle that many $'s.

Chez Rene was beyond my expectations. My husband and I were seated in a quiet corner booth while a tuxedo clad musician played relaxing melodies on a piano across the room. We ordered appetizers, French entrees, and even dessert. Wayne spared no expense. It was definitely worth every $.

As the waiter came to ask if we were ready for the bill, I replied, "Yes, and we would like the senior discount, please." He looked as if I had said I found a severed finger in my food and wanted my meal complimentary. He tried to say he wasn't aware of any senior discount. I had hoped it wouldn't be necessary, but I pulled out the copy of the discounted offer I had printed from the Internet. There it was in black and white *40% senior discounts on Wednesday's dinner service.*

My husband, never the one to haggle, pretended he was seated by sheer happenstance next to a complete stranger like on an AMTRAK dining car. Feeling alone and intimidated in that leather-covered booth with tapered candle light revealing my ever reddening face, I was determined not to pay full $$$$.

The waiter returned and apologized saying they did have a senior discount, but very few patrons ever asked for it. He would, however, have to card me. Card me? Actually, he said something about having to see some identification to make sure I was old enough. Old enough?

I turned around to see who had noticed I was being carded to make sure I was a senior citizen. I paused to remember the last time many years ago when someone asked to see some I.D. It was also to make sure I was old enough to do something. Questioning my mature appearance bruised my youthful pride then; it bolstered my senior pride now. Vanity never is far away, even for discounts.

I suggest a great way to rationalize using coupons to save on eating out: you can use the money you saved to hit the sales at the mall. Just because we're *senior* ladies that doesn't mean we can't look great. Have you seen Sophia Loren lately?

WORDS OF WISDOM: "Give me enough food to live on, neither too much nor too little. If I'm too full, I might get independent, saying, 'God? Who needs him?' If I'm poor, I might steal and dishonor the name of my God." Proverbs 30: 8 - 9

****

"Friendship is born at that moment when one person says to another, 'What! You too? I thought I was the only one." C. S. Lewis

TO FRIEND OR UNFRIEND

∞ 6 ∞

*T*here is a saying that goes, "You can't pick your family, but you can pick your friends." That is sage wisdom as you wind down the years. It's all right to have loads of friends when you're young because you have time on your side to distinguish the true ones from the fair weather ones. Although you have the luxury of time with many things in retirement, I wanted to make friends fast.

If I left the social aspect of our lives to my husband, he would probably be satisfied to live in one of the eco-friendly, grass covered, igloo shaped homes in the middle of nowhere. . . as long as it had cable television capability. When I ask Wayne what happened to the days when you could just run next door and borrow a cup of sugar or feel comfortable asking a neighbor to help you move something heavy, he always has the same answer: "Honey, all I need for a friend is you."

I don't want to hurt his feelings, but I need more friends than just my husband. I love him, but he really doesn't care to discuss which dress stores have Senior Day discounts or the advantages of hormone replacement therapy. I'm certain I heard this somewhere, probably on the Dr. Phil show, that most women need women friends significantly more than most men need men friends. For me, that is a no-brainer.

I'm not sure why, but making friends as I grew older seemed much more complicated and required more energy than I expected to expend. After years of experiencing the good and bad times with old friends, I intuitively knew when things were not right as soon as I heard the sound of their voices. I developed a history of understanding what my friends meant by more than just the words spoken.

Like when my best friend would say on the telephone "Bozo is home," we would laugh because I knew it was her crazy term of endearment for her husband. I understood and didn't take her harmless reference seriously because I had witnessed the love they had for each other through the years. You had to be real, authentic, and just plain you with seasoned friends because they knew when you were not being real, and the best of your friends would confront you about it. At this stage in life, consider yourself lucky if you can count on one hand these kinds of friends.

I decided that friends were an essential element to our happiness and well-being as retirees. It wasn't that Wayne was opposed to doing things occasionally with others, he was just perfectly satisfied with the status quo (just the two of us), and if we connected with another couple by chance, fine. He was not going on any friend hunt with me.

I wasn't asking him to wear a sign after the church service that said: **Would you be our friends, please.** However, his reluctance to even get on board my friend ship cruise was disappointing. It was no easy feat to select another husband and wife to become friends with you and your husband when your own husband wanted nothing to do with the selection process.

I only knew how to make friends the old way: spend time together, see if you and the other wife have common interests, hope that the husbands hit it off well together, and that process took too much time. There had to be a way to streamline the process.

I heard that these young computer whizzes know how to make hundreds of friends with just a click of a button. The time element was not a factor using this method. If there was no friend match after a few computer chats, a person could simply unfriend them on Facebook faster than they could can say "bye-bye" with just the push of a computer key. Puff, they're off her list of friends and out of her life. No excuses, no confrontations, not any embarrassing face to face break-up dramas. It's a painless (insensitive?) way to erase a potential friend before a great deal of time has been expended.

So I made a suggestion to my husband. Perhaps I could develop a system to prequalify potential friends or *friend them* like on the Internet through a thoughtfully designed elimination process similar to the currently popular dating sites. That way we would be in control by making sure other couples were compatible with us. First of all, I might check off any people who have a lot more fun than we do. It would be acceptable to have as much fun or less fun than we do, but they must not have more fun. The reason is simple: doubts will creep in when I begin to wonder why I never noticed how boring my marriage was before.

As an illustration, what if another couple had been selected as finalists at the neighborhood Country Club's version of "Dancing with the Stars" while I'm sitting with my husband on the couch watching a Lawrence Welk rerun, that would be a sure sign not to get too friendly. Don't bother mentioning the couple's expertise on the dance floor to test their friendship potential with your husband. He will just give you another one of those *what are you talking about* looks and say "Who would want to do that?"

My husband saw absolutely no rationale in my second requirement to never have as a friend a woman who still runs in races. My thinking was that she will be so slim that she can always find clothes on sale at Coldwater Creek because all the larger sizes, like I need, are the first to go. Runners also can eat anything they want. Don't do this to yourself. Just like the fun requirement factor but in reverse, pick a friend who is at least your size, bigger is even better.

Financially challenged couples must be walked, no run, away from as soon as humanly possible. They are easy to identify. They are the ones who say, "I'll get it next time." There will never be a next time with them. You will notice they tell the waiter as he prepares to bring the bill, "Don't bother with separate checks. Just split it six ways." Mr. and Mrs. I. M. Cheap have ordered the most expensive appetizer, salads, soups, lobsters, desserts, and a bottle of wine (which only the two of them drank) while the other four had dinner specials with water and no desserts.

That's another thing my husband and I don't see eye to eye about. When most wives go out to eat together, the dining bill is mathematically calculated so that each woman involved pays exactly the amount she owes. It is an unspoken rule women understand. My husband would probably say to the waiter as he brings the bill, "I'll get it." It doesn't seem to bother him that others are not so generous; therefore, wives must run interference. Cut your losses, move on, and always check your caller I.D. so you never have to answer a call from the Cheaps and make excuses why you you're unavailable to eat out with them again.

Historical information was another factor in the friendship selection process. Of course, it would be inevitable for your new acquaintances to enjoy talking about their pre-retirement life. What they did for a living, experiences that were life changing for them, and people who made an indelible mark on who they became as a person are appropriate self disclosures necessary in understanding one another and establishing a new friendship.

We found, unfortunately, those who were stuck in the twilight zone, not in the past, not in the present. Called the "usetas," they are also easy to spot. They continually begin their stories with, "When we were in Minnesota, we use ta..." or "I use ta have a best friend who came over every morning and we..." or "Every day of my life until I retired I use ta..." and "I use ta plant a vegetable garden every year, and this is how I did it..."

They can never come to grips with the fact that life has changed. They retired from their past working life for whatever the reason but can't accept and embrace the different challenges and opportunities essential for a great life as a retiree. I wouldn't want to completely unfriend them because they really need a new friend who will come alongside, take their arm, and help them step into this new world.

We eventually discovered that finding great friends in retirement was only as hard as we chose to make it. In our transient culture, statistics suggest large percentages of people contemplating retirement intend on relocating either to downsize from larger homes or to seek a climate more congenial for senior health and welfare issues. Translate that to mean: we need to make new friends unless we want to be stuck in "usetaland."

A great friend match means not having to try so hard to find common interests. Real keepers should be fun to be around and have many of the same hobbies and interests you enjoy. The beliefs, character, and integrity of others which mirror our own make great connections on the senior citizen version of Friend.com. We still enjoy being around former military couples because we have so many shared experiences about duty stations, and deployments, and can laugh about the complexities of making decision without orders from Headquarters.

A new friend of mine demonstrated the perfect way to befriend someone. She made the effort. In fact, lots of efforts. She invited me to have lunch with her (Dutch treat). She asked me to come to her home to meet the women in her book club. She asked me to meet her at a Bible study for women at a local church. She found out my interests and helped me locate opportunities to further them. Finally, she suggested we go out to dinner and include our husbands. Even though she was *just a little* smaller than me, and she had lots of fun in her life, I knew we would become good friends because she excelled in that wise saying: "To have a friend, you have to be one." Retired or not, that's how friendship is done.

WORDS OF WISDOM: "It's better to have a partner than go it alone. Share the work, share the wealth.

And if one falls down, the other helps. But if there's no one to help, tough! ... By yourself you're unprotected. With a friend, you can face the worst. Can you round up a third? A three-stranded rope isn't easily snapped."

Ecclesiastes 4: 9 - 12

"Our grandchildren accept us for ourselves without rebuke or effort to change us, as no one in our entire lives has ever done, not our parents, siblings, spouses, friends - and hardly ever our own grown children."

Ruth Goode

I'M NANA, HE'S PAPA

⚭⑥⚭

*M*y grandfather, my father, and most fathers of our Baby Boomer generation, worked long and hard at their chosen professions. Men coming home after work and helping their wives cook, clean, fold laundry, give the kids a bath, and put them to bed is a modern phenomenon brilliantly maneuvered by the smarter-than-I-was wives of today. I can count on one hand the number of times Wayne came home from work early enough to give our kids a bath when they were toddlers. Even if he were home at bath time, I never considered asking him to take part in that daily ritual. In those early days of our marriage, I couldn't even picture Wayne sitting on the bathroom floor, being splashed with soapy water while washing little faces and bottoms, then negotiating their wet, slippery torsos out of the tub, to finally dry them off and stuff their gyrating bodies into pajamas. He could lead hundreds, even thousands, of Marines into battle, but bathing four squirming kids was not something he volunteered to do. The house and kids were my job, and I never questioned that arrangement.

We began playing with a different set of rules once we became retired grandparents. The moment that the front door abruptly swings open and shouts of "Nana and Papa" reverberate through the peace and serenity of our home, it is an equal opportunity environment. There was a brief period of transition or denial when Papa thought he would only have to push his grandkids on the swings for a little while or let them help him in the yard, and then he could go sit down and read the newspaper. That was when Nana explained to Papa his new job description. It went something like this:

As a grandfather you will be expected to:

- read story books to any grandchild on request
- answer all questions, i.e. why don't you have hair on top of your head
- run alongside grandchildren while they practice riding two-wheel bikes

- never leave them unattended while you nap even if you say it was only for two minutes
- take them to the playground and go down the sliding board the first time with them
- participate in the care, feeding, and bathing of all grandchildren
- give Nana a break as she's been there and done that, and it's your turn
- be ready and willing to do whatever is necessary to teach your grandchildren the values of honesty, integrity, and morality

Although Wayne accepted this new role with his typical enthusiasm and willingness, keeping up with babies and preschoolers all day can drain the energy bucket dry. Wayne and I feel blessed to see our grandchildren several times a month, but some of our friends and neighbors watch grandchildren on a regular basis every day or at least several times each week. We love our grandchildren and would sacrifice our lives to keep them safe; but short of that, we decided not to give up living our lives so we could be available to babysit every day.

A lively and emotional discussion added some sizzle to a senior citizen's get together at our church recently. Some retirees asked for prayer after feeling especially lethargic. It seemed this condition occurred immediately after keeping the grandchildren for extended periods of time. That's when the sparks began to fly as grandparents hotly debated their role as keepers of the grandkids.

The Keepers group of seniors sincerely believed that this time in a retired couples' life was to be devoted to being the greatest grandparents in the modern world. They kept the grands frequently during the week and almost every weekend to give the kids' parents a break. It was a reasonable and magnanimous gesture of love and concern. These grandparents offered a powerful argument: it was not easy when both parents had to work full time to be able to afford the two luxury cars, a home with a pool in a gated community, and the astronomical prices they had to pay for those fitness club memberships.

How could any grandparent worth their Metamucil not be willing to give up every day to help their adult children out? The little darlings kept them young, they claimed. Besides, their adult sons and daughters would become indignant and quit speaking to them if Grandma and Grandpa wanted to do something on their own and couldn't babysit the grandchildren. Peace at all costs was essential.

The Non Keepers, on the other side of the picket fence, were the seniors who stated their opposing opinions frankly and unapologetically. "I raised my kids with no help from my parents, and I told them before they had any grandkids that I was not about to be the babysitter for anyone else." The Non Keepers argued that most adult children believe their retired parents had little quality of life anyway, and the oldsters would love nothing better than to chase all six of their grandchildren around the neighborhood pool and playground for the whole week end. There are few things more unnerving than a room full of senior citizens loudly disagreeing with each other about their grandchildren.

Like most decisions in life, there are few absolutes. The best decisions are the ones that work for you. Wayne and I wanted to live around our children and have an active role in the lives of our grandchildren. However, we never wanted to feel that being a grandparent and pursuing our own interests were mutually exclusive activities. Love and guilt are incompatible emotions. Love for your grandchildren should not be equated by the number or frequency of times you babysit them or the toys you buy them. They will remember the quality, not quantity, of caring.

Growing up, I only visited my maternal grandmother, Mawmaw, in the mountains of North Carolina once a year, yet her influence on me as a woman is profound. She would sit in her rocking chair, long gray hair rolled up in a tight, neat bun, always in a belted dress, hose, and low heeled shoes and how she loved jewelry! She called me "Gwendolyn" and would laugh when I begged for her to tell me about how she got married in her teen years and had sixteen children.

I have never known a woman as kind, gentle, and accepting as Mawmaw. She didn't have much in material wealth, but what she gave me was much more valuable. She gave unconditional acceptance. I never remember a critical word from her about anyone. I believed nothing I could do would make her stop loving me. She died at almost ninety-five years old. I didn't see her as often as I wanted in her last years, but whenever I called and tried to excuse my absences she would always reply, "Don't you think a thing about it. I know you're busy. I'm just happy to hear your voice."

I'm encouraged that our grandchildren will have great memories of Nana and Papa, too, when I see Wayne holding each grandchild on his lap as he makes wide circles around the six acres on the riding lawn mower, pulling them around on rubber floats in the swimming pool, and, yes, giving them baths. We believe in listening, hugging and loving. That's the kind of grandparents we want our grandchildren to remember when they think of us.

WORDS OF WISDOM: "Your job is to speak out on the things that make for solid doctrine. Guide older men into lives of temperance, dignity, and wisdom, into healthy faith, love, and endurance. Guide older women into lives of reverence so they end up as neither gossips nor drunks, but models of goodness. By looking at them, the younger women will know how to love their husband and children, be virtuous and pure, keep a good house, be good wives. We don't want anyone looking down on God's Message because of their behavior. Also, guide the young men to live disciplined lives." Titus 2: 1 - 6

****

"When you are a child someone gives up part of his life to nurture and sustain you. As an adult, you wrestle with issues that range from diapering and first steps to graduations, weddings, and learning to let go. And now, when it is time for you to care for your parents, you feel like a child again. Going it alone on this journey is impossible. You cannot do it. But each day, with God as your guide, miracles can happen." Myra R. Smith

THE SANDWICH GENERATION
(First slice)

ADULT CHILDREN....seniors....AGING PARENTS.
ADULT CHILDREN

✍️🌀✍️

*A*fter forty-one years of having at least one of our four children at home with us, our youngest child went away to live on a college campus. As she left, I recalled more than twenty years to 1986 when our oldest daughter left for the University of Georgia. I cried all the way from Athens, Georgia, to eastern North Carolina. I did not cry when the last one left. I wondered why all these mothers went into a depression because of an empty nest syndrome. I was thinking: bring that empty nest on!

Wayne, on the other hand, reacted differently than I expected. If you looked up the definition for *overprotection* in the dictionary, there would be a picture of my husband there. Preparing to send our last child off to college, he bought one complete aisle in the snack section of the grocery store so she would have something to eat while at school. He bought a refrigerator for her dorm room so our daughter could load up on drinks, luncheon meat, and anything else cold. He bought bread, peanut butter, jelly, cookies, power bars, and potato chips. He bought a year's supply of razor blades, shampoo, deodorant, pencils, paper, and pens.

I tried to explain to Wayne that we were paying a hefty sum of money so our daughter could eat her meals in the university cafeteria every day. She was not going to the Gulag Archipelago where she would have to forage for food in the frozen tundra. After we unloaded her survival gear from the U Haul trailer, went to the bookstore to buy all her books and even more pens, pencils, and paper, opened a local checking account for her, and sampled a meal in the cafeteria to make certain it was edible, she was begging us to leave.

Afterthefirstmonth, Wayne's calls to our daughter decreased to a reasonable number, five or six a day. We settled in as empty nesters, and I tasted freedom. Along with freedom, Wayne and I tasted the food in just about every restaurant in town. This was a typical scenario several times a week: Wayne suggested we go out for breakfast. We grabbed a quick lunch while we were out on a day trip somewhere. Then I asked Wayne what he wanted for dinner, and he told me not to bother with cooking that we could just go out for dinner. Since cooking was not my favorite activity anyway, eating out suited me just fine.

Wayne and I were having such great times travelling places when our daughter left that I thought the time was finally right for us to discuss our transportation situation. The mileage on our Korean-made sedan was well past a hundred thousand miles and beginning to cost us more every month on repairs and maintenance. Then there was our daughter's Korean-made SUV that she did not take to college. I reasoned to Wayne that we could trade both of those cars in and get a really nice car for once. He was against that idea. He argued that we should keep both of them "...they still had a lot of good miles on them." I used a wife's most powerful ploy: what if the car broke down, and I was alone, at night, with no way to get help.

We drove away from the car lot with a previously owned, low mileage pearl white Cadillac and waved good-bye to our Korean vehicles. I was driving the luxury car I never thought I would own when chocolate cookies and fruit punch drinks covered the back seat of my station wagon. Wayne mentioned that our daughter wouldn't have a car to drive when she came home from school, but that didn't bother me at all as I was confident she would be able to buy her own car once she graduated with a college degree and got a great job. I was wrong.

The boomerang kids, after graduating from college and coming back home to live, brought the reality of a decreased job market right into our own homes. We knew it wasn't our daughter's fault that she couldn't find a job as soon as she graduated. However, her unexpected re-entry into our quiet, orderly home meant we had to learn to play a different game with that retirement deck of cards we were breaking in. Good bye "Solitaire"; hello "Go Fish" for a job!

When our daughter returned home after graduation from college, we thought it would be for just a few weeks until she found work and moved into her own apartment. Weeks and months passed as she applied for jobs without any success. Wayne and I knew she was searching everywhere for companies that were hiring, but hundreds of other unemployed college graduates were also applying for those same positions. We wondered if the retirement life we experienced briefly was over. We weren't eating out as much, and someone else's lifestyle was gradually usurping our retired lives.

Wayne said he understood what it must be like living in a commune. Although there were only three adults living in the house together, the walls started closing in on me. Daytime and nighttime routines become nonexistent. Midnight, these boomerangs insisted, was the optimum period of the day to go on the Internet to fish for jobs. So, of course, staying up to the wee hours of the morning checking out each employment website was so exhausting no one could possibly have expected them to get up before ten o'clock in the morning.

A family is there for each other through good times and bad, but what about the television? We were willing to compromise, but how much could anyone watch reality shows detailing obnoxious events in the lives of spoiled starlets? Wayne wanted me to tell our daughter to turn on the television shows he normally watched like Fox News, get off the Internet, clean her room, turn off all the lights in the house before she went to bed, go to bed earlier, and get up earlier. I tried to explain that his little girl was well over twenty-one years old, and we couldn't tell her what time to go to bed or what television shows to watch. Wayne suggested she join the Marine Corps as they would have no trouble telling her what time to go to bed or anything else.

My decision to sell our daughter's car wasn't such a great idea after all. Wayne said she had to wait until she actually landed a job before he would even think about helping her buy a car. That way she could make the payments and obtain her own auto insurance. Since she did not become employed right away, she had to ride around in an "old person's car" as she called it. I reminded her that the commercials claim a Caddy is not your father's car anymore, while her father reminded her that this one was *his* car.

I'm certain our daughter was not overjoyed with hanging out so much with her boring parents. I told her I realized we weren't much fun since we quit bungee jumping. She didn't think I was very funny either. We kept expecting a silver lining behind the storm clouds, but the monsoon season continued.

After months of applying to Fortune 500 companies without even a response, Wayne just wanted our daughter to get a job anywhere she could. I argued she should continue praying and pursuing a way to use her gifts and talents to help others and honor God. Wayne believed earning a decent wage could be God-honoring, too.

We were both right in a way. I conceded our daughter should continue actively searching for a job, but I didn't want her to give up exploring opportunities off the beaten path. Our daughter, who had always been a gifted artist, decided to use her passion to begin a ministry in children's evangelism. Would she become wealthy as an artist? Probably not, but to witness the joy and excitement in her spirit when involved in her true passion was priceless for me. Watching her reminded me how awesome following your dreams can feel.

Perhaps our sedate, all-too-predictable, life could stand a little more passion as we remembered dreams don't have an age limit for us either. While commiserating with other retired parents about the U turn in our retirement plans after our adult kids returned home, we knew that her constant company was a temporary gift. Soon our daughter, along with her crazy routine, undefeatable spirit, and contagious laughter would follow the path God had designed for her. We would have our time alone again, the quiet would return, we could watch whatever we wanted on the television, and eat out more often...**Empty Nest, The Sequel** promised to be better than the first.

WORDS OF WISDOM: "Oh listen, dear child – become wise...Listen with respect to the father who raised you, and when your mother grows old, don't neglect her. Buy truth – don't sell it for love or money; buy wisdom, buy education, buy insight. Parents rejoice when their children turn out well; wise children become proud parents. So may your father happy! Make your mother proud!" Proverbs 23: 21 – 25

****

"When I was little my grandfather used to make me stand in a closet for five minutes without moving. He said it was elevator practice." Stephen Wright

THE SANDWICH GENERATION
(Second slice)

ADULT CHILDREN....seniors....AGING PARENTS.
AGING PARENTS

*A*t a shopping center located near a retirement community, I observed what appeared to be a caretaker daughter with a cane, assisting her mother on a walker out of a car and into the grocery store. I laughed when I heard the ninety-something-year-old mother complaining to her seventy-something-year-old daughter as they were getting out of their car, "If you don't stop driving so fast, I'm going to take the car keys away from you."

If that situation involved my mother and me, I would be the one telling her to slow down or I would take away the keys to her car. She has always driven like she was practicing for the Indianapolis 500. In her late eighties, she lives in a small mountainous area in western North Carolina. You can only reach her mountaintop town by maneuvering thirty to forty-five minutes of nerve racking, white knuckling curves. There are two ways up and down the mountain, one road leads to and from Asheville, and the other road leads to and from Atlanta.

Wayne and I snaked our way up and down these roads in every season. Breathtaking mountains resplendent in fall colors, waterfalls cascading into winding creek beds, and spring mornings when mountain tops peek through the fog covering the low lying areas like clouds make each trip a spectacular scenic tour. The periodic snows have been brutal, and the leafless trees and monotonous grey skies continue for a seemingly endless winter. We always respected the beauty and danger of the mountains, but my mother never feared of anything.

I rarely heard my husband in an argument with anyone except me. To his credit, he never, and I do mean *never,* in our forty-five years of marriage, started even a heated discussion with me. If he disagreed with something I had said, he did it in a respectful, courteous manner. I, on the other hand, felt compelled to get upset at him because of something he had done or failed to do like promising to straighten out the garage and then forgetting to do it. I was justified in starting those arguments. However, my little white-haired mother brought out a side of my husband that no one else had been able to do.

We've heard people should not debate religion and politics if they wanted to stay on speaking terms. That's good advice. However, Wayne and my mother didn't listen to those pearls of wisdom. They seemed to butt heads together on only those two topics every time they got together. My mother knows a great deal about the Bible and was a well-respected Bible teacher through the years. Wayne was a diligent, knowledge-able teacher of Biblical truths in many churches.

Their disagreements usually began innocently enough. For example, Wayne read an article in one of my mother's monthly magazines for senior adults and commented that some studies cited in the article reveal wine, in moderation, might have a positive impact on the heart. My mother countered with, "I've never had a drop of alcohol in my whole life." Wayne pointed out that various scriptures mentioned wine being consumed such as Jesus turning water into wine at a wedding and the apostle Paul's advising Timothy to drink a little wine for the stomach's sake. My mother adamantly maintained those incidents referred to grape juice. Neither was willing to concede that the other might be right in any way, but at least the discussion was civil.

Civilized was not the word I used when the elephant and donkey suddenly appeared, took seats at my mother's kitchen table, and invited my mother and Wayne to join them. Wayne and my mother could not be further polarized in the political world. Wayne insisted there was a term used to describe my mother and her political persuasion: Yellow Dog. I never knew what that meant until I asked one of my uncles who lived up in the mountains. "Why, that just means it wouldn't matter if your mama's political party put up a yellow dog for election, your mama would vote for the dog rather than the other party's candidate." I think my mother said that Hound Dog would describe Wayne's political persuasion.

Whenever talk between my mother and Wayne got around to political parties or candidates, I tried to get out of the line of fire and leave the room. My mother usually talked about the party she did not support as though that party's elected officials were responsible for every evil deed ever done in the history of the world. Wayne would then forcefully point out the errors in my mother's opinions which never set well with his mother-in-law. They went at it as though the next election would be decided right then and there by whoever was victorious in his or her arguments.

Wayne told me whenever we left to go home, "Your mother is so stubborn. She thinks she knows everything about politics." My mother got me aside before we left and said, "Your husband thinks just because he worked at the Pentagon he knows everything about Washington, D. C. Well, I know a thing or two, myself." Other than religious interpretations and opinions about politics, they got along remarkably well.

Although my mother is feisty, independent, and drives too fast around those mountain curves, there will be a time, if God lets her live long enough, when she will need some help. We know that my mother will not want to move from what is familiar to her, and we knew we would not make a permanent move to the mountains of North Carolina. We, along with many other retirees, continue to be faced with this dilemma: how do we become parents to our parents?

Sociologists and psychologists tell us the happiest people are the ones who feel they still have choices in how they live their lives. When we presented a carefully designed plan to my mother about bringing someone in to help her occasionally, she flatly refused the offer. She insisted she didn't need anyone to help her, and that she was absolutely capable of taking care of herself. She told us, "I've prayed about it, and God will let me know when the time comes to get some help." It was difficult to dispute her agreement with God, but Wayne said he would feel more confident if he heard God's side of that conversation with my mother.

We continue to visit my mother frequently and monitor her welfare with other relatives who live close to her. Wayne proved through the years that he was ready and willing to contribute time, money, and hours of travel to ensure my mother was honored in her old age. Many husbands were not so cooperative. I saw marriages dissolve because husbands were not willing to spend their retirement years accommodating live-in mothers-in-law.

Wayne and I lived our lives with gusto, and we want our children and grandchildren to celebrate every day of their lives without worrying what to do with Dad when he starts wearing socks with sandals or with Mom when she wants to cook all the time but forgets to turn off the stove. We explained our choices to our children about how we wanted to handle our end-of-life care. Although our children were hesitant and uncomfortable talking about this, there might come the time when Wayne and I won't be able to live alone. What will happen to us in the future is still a mystery. There is, however, something we know for certain: there will be an end of life for us. Unless the Lord comes back first, we will be absent here on earth as we move into eternity.

I discovered many truths becoming the filling in this sandwich generation. I realized that to honor others I must be willing to listen to what they choose for their lives. I determined not to take on the role of a co-dependent for anyone by assuming that their problems were my problems, too. I found out the hard way that no one is ever happy when he or she is forced to do anything against their will, parents or children. Wayne gently reminds me that I must let the ones I love live their own lives.

Perhaps the greatest lesson I learned was that every one of my actions will have definite consequences. The Bible calls it the *principle of sowing and reaping.* Whatever we sow in life, good or bad, we will reap: **in like kind, more of, and later than** the action, thought or word we have sowed. If I am concerned first and foremost with my own welfare and care nothing for others who are hurting, I know what my future will hold. Someday I might be the second slice on a sandwich myself.

So if you have to be a part of the sandwich generation, choose to be an Oreo. It is the perfect combination: a sweet harmony of flavors with the outside crunchy chocolate layer cookies held deliciously together by just the right amount of the absolutely essential creamy middle. Everyone knows that when it is appropriate, you can remove the middle (a.k.a. "… the kid will eat the middle of an Oreo first") and the chocolate cookie ends can be great all on their own.

WORDS OF WISDOM: "Don't be misled: No one makes a fool of God. What a person plants, he will harvest. The person who plants selfishness, ignoring the needs of others – ignoring God! - harvests a crop of weeds. All he'll have to show for his life is weeds! But the one who plants in response to God, letting God's Spirit do the growth work in him, harvests a crop of real life, eternal life." Galatians 6: 7 – 8.

****

"Don't ever question the value of volunteers. Noah's Ark was built by volunteers; the Titanic was built by professionals." Unknown

VOLUNTEERISM

☙ ⑥ ☙

"*T*wenty-three volunteer jobs!" I was in the checkout line at a dress shop recently and began talking with the lady in front of me as we compared our retirement experiences. She mentioned that she had a part time job, but her husband was never at home because of all his volunteer activities. He actually volunteered for twenty-three different organizations. He began his habit of extravagant good deeding by offering to help with security around their fifty-five-plus community. After a few months, he was "promoted" to head of security which meant he had a uniform and a specially designated golf cart.

I imagined someone attempting mischief would not have to be an Olympic sprinter to outrun a golf cart with a senior citizen at the wheel. He also went scuba diving once a week at the aquarium as a volunteer to clean out the fish poop (fish feces?) She was just getting started with his laundry list of volunteer assignments, when it was her turn to check out. Whew...I was getting tired just listening to all her husband accomplished in a week.

As I drove home, I began mulling over what she had told me. If her husband had twenty-three volunteer jobs, he had to be out of the house almost every day. A husband out of the house and doing something worthwhile for others would be perfect for me, I mean my husband. Now I just had to decide what worthwhile charity organizations could use Wayne's skills and talents.

Since living on our six-acre property, Wayne had kept himself extremely busy painting fences, mowing, maintaining the fields, and hauling off truck loads of limbs that were constantly falling from the over one-hundred-plus year-old granddaddy oaks that I thought were so beautiful when I first saw this property. I was confident that Wayne had a burning desire to do more than just maintenance work, and that he was only pretending to be content.

I began Internet searches on possible volunteer opportunities that I thought would fit well with Wayne's background and work experience. I did an inventory of his past jobs. He was an Infantry Officer in the Marine Corps, he was accustomed to being in command, he was great at war strategy and tactics, and he received leadership awards consistently throughout his career. I thought he would be perfect to be on the board of directors of some non-profit organization or to head up a fund raising campaign for a major charity. When I finally suggested to Wayne that we both should start thinking about giving back to the community, he was in full agreement, almost.

I was surprised to learn that he had been thinking about volunteering, too. He hadn't mentioned it to me, and I began to wonder if there might be other things Wayne had not mentioned to me about what he wanted to do in retirement. But the discussion about what *he* wanted could be saved for another day, as I was eager to share the opportunities I had selected for him to either sit on boards or strategize fund raising events.

Wayne listened and then said, "No, I don't want to do those things." It startled me for a minute because I thought I had done all my analysis and knew exactly what would be perfect for him. He said that he heard about a local food bank that needed someone in the warehouse to stock the shelves. He wanted to do that. Wayne drove to the faith-based organization that was supported through donations of individuals and local churches, signed up, and began stocking supplies in the warehouse once a week. He inspired me to reassess what I could do to give back.

I went to the local library and discovered there was a need for a Writers' Group. A new enthusiastic, twenty-something librarian asked me to facilitate the group which we decided to call Adventures in Writing. She took the lead and made all the marketing arrangements, advertisements, and flyers, and wrote newspaper articles about the group. She called and emailed me often to make certain I had everything I needed to lead the group. It proved to be one of my most gratifying assignments as I watched the confidence and camaraderie of the group increase from week to week.

I thought I knew what my husband wanted to do when he retired. Many of his contemporary Marine Corps generals were involved with big things: political appointments, consulting with defense contractors, presidents of companies. Immediately after Wayne left the Marine Corps, he became president of a boy's college preparatory high school for six years. After leaving that assignment, he continued to choose big things to do in retirement: leading a Bible study, volunteering at a local food bank, and spending quality time with his family.

After four decades of living with Wayne, I thought I knew everything about my husband. I arrived early to pick him up from the food bank one day. I watched him through the open doors as he worked alone in the warehouse, lifting boxes of canned goods, stacking the shelves. Then he saw me in the car. He waved at me with a big smile on his face. He was happy. I thought as I waved back that maybe this would be a good time to ask him what else *he* wanted to do in retirement. We often forget that there are two sides to every story. Take time to find out the side that isn't yours.

WORDS OF WISDOM: "So – join the company of good men and women, keep your feet on the tried-and-true paths. It's the men who walk straight who will settle this land, the women with integrity who will last here. The corrupt will lose their lives; the dishonest will be gone for good." Proverbs 2: 20 - 22

****

"We don't need to increase our goods nearly as much as scaling down our wants. Not wanting something is as good as possessing it." Donald Horban

DOWNSIZING

❦⑥❦

*W*e collected a lot of stuff during our more than forty years of marriage. After we married in 1966, we moved everything we had in the back of our car to our first apartment at the University of Georgia. Our retirement move took up all the space in a gigantic Atlas moving van. Our total weight was listed at 26,000 pounds or some ridiculously large number. I was almost embarrassed when the driver made me sign the twenty sheets of inventory. We just never threw anything away. Retirement was the time to lighten our load in more ways than one.

"Your trash is someone else's treasure" is a flea market enticement. After offering to give away personal belongings to our children, I concluded a more appropriate slogan would be: your treasure is somebody else's trash. I couldn't believe that the treasures from a lifetime of amassing unique artifacts from around the world like four Japanese wedding kimonos, a petrified rock from the petrified forest, a complete, although tarnished, silver tea service with tray, handmade quilts, a collection of ten antique salt and pepper shakers, a twenty-eight-year-old red tricycle with a slightly bent back wheel, and valuable other treasures too numerous to count would not be grabbed up.

As hard as this might be to believe, our children did not lust over nor have the slightest interest in most of what we considered our treasures. Our kids told us they had enough of their own stuff to give away, they didn't need any more. Over the years I went to more estate sales than I care to remember. An individual's most personal and intimate possessions would be spread out on a lawn as though the house was turned upside down shaking the contents out in disarray, exposed for strangers to pick through. That was not going to be the fate of my stuff. My possessions would have a dignified resting place by my own direction. I began going through each room making piles: dishes to Salvation Army, exercise equipment to a military high school, furniture to Goodwill, books to the local library, special things to keep, and unsalvageable things to the dump. I was so swift, efficient, and organized that I could have produced a YouTube video on how best to downsize after retirement.

Then Wayne walked in and asked the question I had learned to dread, "What are you doing with this?" I knew what was coming next. "You can't give that away. We bought that when we went to see Custer's last stand back in 1978. That coffee cup has a lot of memories for me." It didn't matter that the manila discolored mug was chipped and you could hardly tell whether there was Gen. Custer's or Sitting Bull's picture on the side, he pulled it out of the "dump" pile. That same scenario was repeated constantly as he meandered through my piles pulling things out while I demanded he put them back in the donation piles.

I didn't get it. Most of the articles he insisted he couldn't live without had been packed up in some box or stored away in a closet. After talking to numerous retired wives, I discovered this propensity for a man to keep everything he had ever purchased, touched, or even walked by in the proximity of his home or garage was a universal male obsession named "menilkeepitall."

This personality disorder manifested itself in a bizarre ritual for the male of the species. Being observed, normally by a female caretaker (a.k.a. wife), the patient (a.k.a. husband) exhibited irrational and delusional behavior by insisting that nothing of any perceived or even insignificant value could be removed from a male's premises without his knowledge and consent. That consent is rarely given.

If someone had given me some good *advice* about this strange quirk in men, I would not have blatantly paraded all my *donations* out in the open in neat piles, a move that only intensified the symptoms of menilkeepitall. I had to change my tactics if my downsizing plan was going to work at all. Then it occurred to me, he hadn't thought about most of those memories in years.

It was the "out of sight and out of mind" principle. If I could just get all those things out of his sight, he wouldn't mind that they were even gone. I didn't think I was being devious about properly and sensitively finding new homes for our things because I knew my husband had the disorder and couldn't help himself.

Disposing of my unwanted possessions without Wayne knowing was not going to be an easy feat. He was around most of the time since he retired and not much escaped his notice. I thought about a covert nighttime operation, but most thrift stores were not open 24 hours a day. I decided that my plan had to incorporate patience and diligence.

Whenever I had any hesitations about my downsizing efforts, I remembered those estate sales. I would not have my treasured stuff strewn about a yard with less than sentimental shoppers bartering on the lowest prices for my kimonos. At least, I would have some input into giving my things a fond farewell. I began a staging area in a storage room off the garage for everything I needed to remove.

I was waiting for the perfect opportunity, a window of opportunity, to haul off a carload to the local Salvation Army Thrift Shop. Then my cover was blown. Wayne walked into the kitchen and said, "Honey, why do you have all our things stacked up in the storage room?" Since the best defense is offense, I explained, "Wayne, God would not want us to keep all that stuff that we never use when there are so many hurting people who are in need and would be so thankful to have it.?" Skillful as a tactician, Wayne replied, "Yes, there are lots of homeless people who have been praying for a kimono to wear this winter. Come on. These things mean something to me. I'm sorry you can so easily get rid of significant things that we gathered throughout our life together."

Perhaps I wasn't taking his feelings into consideration. I didn't know he had *sentimental feelings*, at least to that extent, about our things. I agreed to a compromise. We rented a storage unit for everything that I was absolutely certain we would never use again and which had no sentimental value to me but that Wayne wanted to keep. I told him that he could go over and visit his stuff whenever we wanted. It was a fair resolution for both of us. Wayne insisted he should assist me in sorting through my intended give away items to ensure I wasn't disposing of his treasures and that we were donating usable things to charities.

Retirement was a crossroads to me. We were at the junction of a new beginning, an untraveled road ahead that would provide brand new memories and adventures for us. Like all the Snowbirds driving down from their frozen northern homes to soak up our beautiful winter weather here in Florida, I sought their joy of freedom from a lifetime of everyday routines. I assumed they accomplished this free-dom from the norm by temporarily exchanging their perma-nent houses for ones on wheels.

I watched scores of recreational vehicles headed south. Some traveled with just a camper trailer on the bed of their pickup truck, others towed a car or truck behind their bus-sized RV, with several bicycles attached like protruding warts on the back of the bus, and occasionally a motorcycle attached behind all that. I read somewhere there were giant RV's measuring seventy-five feet long, two decks high, with patios on the top. Enough never seemed to be enough for some people.

I wanted to travel light, with just the essentials to accompany us in retirement like the pickups with a pop up camper on the truck bed. The twenty pages of possessions were getting too heavy for me to pull along behind. However, I was not alone on this journey. My traveling companion standing beside me at the crossroads needed to bring along reminders of home with him. Downsizing material possessions should not be accomplished at the expense of downsizing memories. Like good friends, memories are meant to lighten our load, lift our spirits, and enrich our journey. Since a petrified rock achieved the same *friend* effect for Wayne, it remained in the save pile.

WORDS OF WISDOM: "Don't hoard treasure down here where it gets eaten by moths and corroded by rust or – worse! – stolen by burglars. Stockpile treasure in heaven, where it's safe from moth and rust and burglars. It's obvious, isn't it? The place where your treasure is, is the place you will most want to be, and end up being." Matthew 6: 19 -21

****

ZOE'S ZUMBA CLASS

"When I was young I was called a rugged individualist. When I was in my fifties I was considered eccentric. Here I am doing and saying the same things I did then and I'm labeled senile." George Burns

FIT AS A FIDDLE AFTER FIFTY

❧ ⑥ ❧

*T*he telltale signs were there. Clothes were mysteriously shrinking in my closet, and my rings were becoming so tight I could barely get them off my fingers. I attributed it to the fact that the humidity in Florida was making my body swell. I was certain those hot, sticky summer days were the reason for my weight gain, too, because most of my senior women friends were complaining of the same symptoms. Unfortunately, the low humidity and cooler temperatures of winter did not alleviate the problem.

I was not going to accept the fact that I was just plain getting f_t. I couldn't bring myself to even say the word that was defined as an unhealthy increase in body mass. I asked Wayne if he thought I was gaining weight. I've used many adjectives to describe my husband through the years, but stupid was not one of them. He looked at me as though what I had just asked was the most absurd question ever uttered and said, "Of course not, Honey, you look as good as you ever did." It might have been the way the light was shining, but I believe his nose grew a little longer after he said that.

My husband had no trouble keeping in great physical shape before he retired. He was a Marine for almost forty years. He ate whatever he wanted and exercised on a daily basis. Discipline was his middle name. He broke the World's Sit-Up record when he was forty years old by completing forty thousand consecutive sit-ups without stopping. I told the truth when I said he was disciplined.

After Wayne retired, eating out so often had put a couple of extra pounds on his six pack stomach, too. Although he still looked great to me, I suggested that we should start exercising consistently and being more careful about what we ate, for our health, of course. Wayne's favorite thing to do was working out at the gym, so he was in complete agree-ment with me. He said he would come up with an exercise plan if I would design the meal plan.

I admitted I needed a plan I could stick with through the years. I noticed there was a weight management program at a nearby senior community center. I went to a meeting. It began and one of the senior ladies related how depressed she was because she had gained three pounds the previous week. She detailed her strict diet, how she had survived on mostly carrots and low calorie food most of the day, and how she had tried to exercise more. I was disillusioned by the time I heard her story.

Eating out was one of the best parts of being retired. Wayne and I didn't go on exotic vacations or go dancing at the country club, so I had to ask myself: was losing weight all that important to me anyway? I debated the feasibility of buying an entire new wardrobe, but a frugal voice in my head whispered, "That's a crazy thing to do. Just lose the weight."

There had to be a way that I could have my cake and lose weight, too. Maybe if I just exercised more, I could still eat out sometimes. While Wayne worked out with weights at a local fitness center, I decided to check out the group exercises. I told myself that joining other women in an exercise class was a great way to socialize, meet potential friends with the same interests, and get in shape. I signed up for a Zumba class, whatever that was, but it sounded fun to me. I read the description: Latin-inspired dance fitness program, easy to follow dance moves, ditch the workout and join the party...just the kind of exercise routine I could learn to love.

Entering the Zumba classroom, I noticed there were no other seniors. If any woman was over fifty-five years old, that Zumba was really working because they all looked in awesome shape. I've always been a good dancer and had some pretty good moves in my day, so I wasn't worried about keeping up. How hard could it be to shake it up to a Latin beat?

The instructor, Brandi, walked into the room wearing tight hot pink spandex shorts, a black halter top, and a headpiece microphone. I'd seen the pastor in our church use the same device when he gave his sermons, not in the same outfit, of course. High tech had entered the exercise world since my last Jazzercise class thirty years ago.

Brandi skipped over to the huge black radio, pushed a button, and the walls in the room began to gyrate from the volume and intensity of the music. Now I understood why she had to wear that microphone so we could hear her over that noise. The regulars in the class must have been doing this Zumba routine for a while because they all seemed to know the steps like choreographed dancers in a New York City music hall. I hadn't seen hips and feet move that fast since a fire drill at the senior center.

Not one to quit anything, I did my best to follow the twenty-year-old girl in front of me who was in perfect step with the instructor. Then there was one hip action too many. As I tried to shake my upper portion and turn with my lover portion, my body revolted. I fell in the middle of all those Radio Music Hall-like dancers. It was the only part of the experience that was in slow motion to me as everyone stopped, looked at me sprawled on the floor, and rushed over to help me up.

Humiliating was an understatement for my ego at that moment. I happened to notice as I was being helped to my feet, that Wayne had finished his workout and was watching the whole debacle through the glass window. He smiled at me. I couldn't tell if it was a "Boy, do you ever look like a fool" or a "Honey, I'm proud of you for trying" smile. I didn't even want to know.

We left the fitness center and returned home. Later that evening I read an article in the newspaper advising seniors that staying slim is one component of longevity. How long did I want to live if I had to give up everything I loved to eat and take another Zumba class? Wayne could tell my ego had taken a big hit at Zumba class and reassured me that I was in much better shape than most of the women my age.

When I checked my emails later, I received a message offering an Internet health indicator test to determine how my overall health translated into my body's real age. I took that test to see if Wayne was right about my being in good shape for my age. The results were sent to me shortly in another email message. There was no way I had the body of an eighty-two-year old! I sent that ridiculous message to my spam account. What does your body know anyway, it's not a brain!

I curled up in the recliner that evening with large, medicinal smelling pads delivering muscle relaxing and pain relieving warmth to my lower back and other Zumba affected body parts. I had almost decided to give up and accept the inevitable. My Zumba days were over. Cutting down on caloric intake would be difficult unless I began cooking at home more. Wayne lost his extra pounds in just a few weeks of exercising consistently and was able to eat what he wanted again, darn it.

It seems to me senior men have a different perspective about body image than their wives. I noticed a group of laughing guys by the neighbor's barbeque grill, shirts off, and oblivious to the fifty or sixty extra pounds encircling their once trim midsections like out of control yeast dough. No shame, no self consciousness, an utterly insignificant factor for their confidence, self esteem, and ego. There has got to be something positive and affirming about accepting yourself, f_t and all.

WORDS OF WISDOM: "Don't you know anything? Haven't you been listening? God doesn't come and go. God lasts. He's Creator of all you can see or imagine. He doesn't get tired out, doesn't pause to catch his breath. And he knows everything, inside and out. He energizes those who get tired, gives fresh strength to dropouts. For even young people tire and drop out, young folk in their prime stumble and fall. But those who wait upon God get fresh strength. They spread their wings and soar like eagles. They run and don't get tired, they walk and don't lag behind." Isaiah 40: 28 – 31.

****

"Use your health, even to the point of wearing it out. That is what it is for. Spend all you have before you die; do not outline yourself." George Bernard Shaw

DR. OZ IS MY PHYSICIAN

A popular philosophy propagated years ago was that all the important lessons in life you learned in kindergarten. Well, everything I needed to know about my health, I learned from Dr. Oz. From the first time I watched his daily medically oriented television show I was hooked. I saw Dr. Oz bring on stage an audience member to lift ten pounds of ugly fat illustrating in graphic terms what I was actually carrying around on my hips. This doc had to be the real deal.

He taught me how to determine if I was dehydrated by pinching the skin on my hand. I also learned that the super fruit, African mango, would help rid my body of those ugly ten pounds of fat. Unfortunately, after buying the fairly expensive pills, I did not magically lose the weight after the expected two weeks. I did not blame Dr. Oz, of course. I was certain the failure to lose was somehow my fault. How could the good doctor ever steer me wrong?

After scores of Dr. Oz observations, I developed some medical theories of my own. One theory was that retirees seemed to be categorized into three main types: those who visited medical offices as frequently as I went to the grocery store, those who believed you were going to die sometime anyway no matter what you did so why bother going to doctors, and those who went to doctors when it was necessary like when your appendix was about to burst. I considered myself in the last category although Wayne would argue I was definitely in the second group.

Another theory of mine proposed that too much money was spent on healing people after they've become sick instead of keeping people from getting sick in the first place. Anyone who approached the magic age of sixty-five could attest to receiving so much Medicare material in the mail that your postman went to the hospital for hernia surgery after the Open Enrollment period was over. I never knew so many people were concerned about my health benefits.

There must be legitimate cause for this concern because I rarely found an available parking spot at the local medical centers and hospitals without driving around for thirty minutes waiting for someone to leave. Fortunately, due to my paranoia of hearing bad news in any form, the parking situation wasn't a problem for me. I seldom darkened the door of a doctor's office.

I never disagreed with those who believed in the dynamic duo of prayer and physicians in restoring health because the Bible informs us someday we will return to dust. Like old cars, our body parts wear out with age. The real problem for me occurred when seniors would not *accep*t that aches and pains come with the territory.

Wayne and I took a neighbor who was in her late eighties to a doctor's appointment recently. She asked me to come in to see the doctor with her as she was hard of hearing. Refusing to get a hearing aid, she said she didn't need one, and that other people just mumbled too much. The doctor was kind, patient, and thorough. The examination seemed to be over as the doctor pushed his stool back.

"You are looking good. No real problems as your tests came out great." I thought my elderly neighbor would be pleased, but the shocked look on her face confused me. Perhaps she hadn't heard him correctly, so I repeated loudly, "He said you look great, and we can go now." She stared at me as if I was hearing impaired.

"I heard what he said. He's crazy. I know there is something wrong with me. I don't feel right." The doctor was concerned as he scooted his stool back towards my neighbor and asked, "Can you tell me where it hurts?" She shook her head, "No, I can't tell you exactly where it hurts, but I know it does somewhere."

After another thirty minutes of trying to diagnose her mysterious illness, the doctor finally told my neighbor that he was sorry but couldn't find anything wrong with her. He told her there were patients waiting for him who were really sick and quickly left the room.

I helped my neighbor out to the reception desk. The secretary asked my neighbor if she needed a follow-up appointment. My neighbor said, "No, I'm never coming back here again. He doesn't know what he's doing. I am sick." It reminded me of the story of a little old lady who was known as a hypochondriac in the town. When she finally died, she had previously made arrangements to put on her tombstone these words: See, I told you I was sick.

Wayne and I took our neighbor home and helped her get settled inside. I told Wayne what happened in the doctor's office. It baffled me why some people convinced themselves they were sick so they had to go to the doctor all the time.

Wayne casually mentioned that he was baffled by other people who talked themselves out of going to the doctor when they really needed to go. I had no idea who he had in mind. In a few days I noticed that there was a significant pain in my right big toe. It became progressively more red and irritated. There was an unexplainable lump protruding from the left side. I instituted my normal procedures: look up all the possible causes of my malady on the Internet, leaf through my family medical books, and panic. By the second week of no improvement despite foot bath soaks with Epsom salts, ointments, and bandages, I had not been able to diagnosis the problem, but I was certain the diagnosis was not going to be good.

Wayne said he could always tell when I was worried about some physical illness because I would try to heal myself through my self-help books. He believed that I had read so much medical information through the years that I could probably perform brain surgery on myself. That was crazy. I would definitely go to see an acupuncture doctor before I did that.

Wayne suggested that I should make an appointment to see a doctor. That was easy for him to say. I told him that I would decide when I needed medical attention. He called me a Big Baby and walked away. That is another thing about retired husbands: what makes them think they have the right to give advice to their wives on everything?

Pre-retirement, I moved into and out of houses by myself, bought and sold real estate by myself, drove across country by myself, and went to the doctor by myself. Once I fell and broke my shoulder. I drove myself to the hospital because Wayne was gone on a training exercise. He might have used many adjectives to describe me through the years, but Big Baby was not one of them.

I had to wear sandals after about three weeks with my toe swollen. Finally, Wayne said that I had to go to a doctor or my toe was going to fall off. His threat was the impetus I needed. I made an appointment with a foot doctor and resigned myself to an unfavorable outcome. Wayne drove me to the appointment and seemed unusually jovial. Perhaps I had been mistaken about how much he enjoyed my company in retirement because he didn't appear to care about the gravity of my situation. The doctor did a foot x-ray and said I had a bone spur. There were several courses of action but probably the most reasonable resolution was just to buy wider shoes. Wider shoes! That was it.

Wayne waited patiently, seemingly immersed in reading a podiatrist monthly magazine, *Putting Your Best Foot*

Forward, or something like that. He looked up at me, put down the magazine, and started walking to the door. I stopped by the receptionist desk to give her my insurance card then followed Wayne to the car. "Well," he said after we buckled our seat belts, "are you going to live?" Men are not good winners and feel the need to gloat whenever they are right. Yes, he told me weeks ago to just go see a doctor and stop the Internet searches and medical book descriptions of all the terrible diseases I probably had. "Come on," I threw back at him, "it was just a big toe." I liked it better when I drove myself to the doctor.

I conceded to Wayne that he was probably right about one thing, visiting a doctor, even for routine check-ups, was a wise thing to do. That's exactly what Dr. Oz would tell me to do. Hey, Dr. Oz challenged me to reboot my body in just two weeks with the Dr. Oz Ultimate Diet. Forget about the African Mango pills, I felt this new weight loss plan was a sure thing.

WORDS OF WISDOM: "…I pray for good fortune in everything you do, and for your good health. 3 John 1:2

"Here is the test to find whether your mission on earth is finished: if you're alive, it isn't." Alice Roosevelt Longworth

RETIRED or REFIRED

❧ ⑥ ❧

R aring to go, on an Internet Google search, would render this definition: one who is full of energy and can't wait to get started on whatever it is they're going to do. I was *raring to go* when we retired. Sitting in an overstuffed recliner with the remote control for the flat screen television in one hand, a cup of coffee in the other hand, and a good book close by on the side table would not be my idea of raring to go.

Others might argue that retirement should be simple and uncomplicated. To me, however, living an exciting and purposeful life was complicated, and relaxation only goes so far until it becomes another word for boredom. Most seniors migrate into one of two directions: retired or refired. Wayne and I had our own opposing definitions for both of those terms.

It was clear that our perceptions of promises made to one another, mainly from Wayne, were grossly misinterpreted, mainly by me. Whenever I complained to Wayne through the years about his not taking enough time off from work for us to go on a vacation, or to go scuba diving after I became a certified diver, or to go snow skiing over the winter holidays, I always received the same response, "Honey, when I retire, we'll have time to do all the things we never had time to do." Much like the, "Honey, you can pick the place" promise, I was a believer again.

When Wayne said, "Honey, when I retire, we'll have time to do all the things we never had time to do," he was basically speaking about all the things he never got to do while earning a living for his family. He amassed an extensive collection of history books through the years. Retirement allowed him uninterrupted time to read for hours. He was a country boy at heart, so he worked outside keeping up the fields and planting a garden. He painted miles of four board fences that surrounded our property and the three paddocks. He bought a record player to use with his collection of old, long-playing records and listened to them in the evenings. He finally was able to do all the things he never had time to do prior to retirement. He was content. My husband and I had different opinions about how to achieve contentment in this season of our lives.

I was going to share my talents by working at something I loved to do, and I was determined to discover what that was. So I set out in my new retiree world to find "it." I became an adjunct instructor of Effective Public Speaking at a community college. Although I had taught at four-year colleges in the past, the community college setting would be a new challenge. Molding and encouraging young minds in any setting would qualify as purposeful, I reasoned.

There were students of all ages in my classes from recent high school graduates to those in their 50s and 60s. I was definitely impressed with the mature individuals coming back for their associate degrees or just to take some classes for self improvement. I fully expected them to be model students, and I was never disappointed.

Some recent high school graduates were another story. One young woman approached me after receiving a grade lower than she expected and complained, "Why do you have the right to determine my grade? I thought my speech was great." I rapidly became disenchanted with molding and encouraging young minds. I gave those community college students my best effort before deciding to let the teaching ship sail on without me. I was assured I would find another opportunity to do all the things I never was able to do before.

After completing more than twenty applications for part time employment and getting nowhere, sitting on the front porch began to look purposeful enough to me. However, contemplating the cloud formations didn't hold my fascination for long as I recalled Joni Mitchell's lyrics from her best selling record *Both Sides Now*,

> *I've looked at clouds from both sides now,*
>
> *from up and down and still somehow.*
>
> *Its cloud illusions I recall.*
>
> *I really don't know clouds at all.*

I was beginning to realize that I didn't really know retirement at all.

Wayne was able to transition into what he wanted to do with such ease, and many of my friends expressed the same sentiment about their husbands. One husband never had enough time to play golf before he retired, so he was on the golf course five mornings every week. Another husband dreamed of opening up a carpentry shop where he could make nativity scenes, rocking horses, and cabinets for his friends. He bought a small building and converted it into his shop. Our neighbor loved antique trucks but never had enough time to work on them until he retired. He and one of his trucks were even on the cover of a local magazine.

Some wives had the opposite situation. Their husbands never had any hobbies or interests before they retired and wanted none after they retired. These desperate wives were losing their minds, and who would blame them. Imagine a man who stayed home everyday wanting to know where his wife was and what she was doing all the time. These were normally the husbands who wanted to micromanage every aspect of their wives' lives, i.e. they checked the dishwasher to make sure it was full enough before letting their wives start it, they stood over the stove to make certain the green beans were not overcooked, they complained that a sixty watt bulb was in the lamp instead of a forty watt bulb. These wives prayed for the hobby angel to appear and bless their husbands with a hobby, preferably something that would keep them out of the house all day, every day.

It seemed fair to me that retirement allowed husbands an opportunity to pursue activities they couldn't do when earning a living and family responsibilities gobbled up their time. I wondered why more women never experienced these epiphanies after retirement. Perhaps those who stayed home while raising their families were more in control of their schedule and how they chose to spend their time, especially as the children became older. I was my own boss and set my own schedule every day while my husband didn't have that freedom or flexibility. He deserved to do whatever he wanted now that he had the opportunity.

So I took the time to think about what I really *wanted* to accomplish in this season of my life. I liked the idea of going scuba diving, and snow skiing, and on exotic vacations when we were younger because I thought that's what families were supposed to do. I decided I didn't care what people were supposed to do in retirement. Everyone should do whatever makes him or her happy. I knew what made me happy. I wanted to be a writer. Someone very wise once said, "If you want to be a writer, write." It may have been my husband; however, it made perfect sense to me.

Wayne read his books or painted his fences while I wrote. He was supportive of my desire to sit in front of a computer for hours and just write. Occasionally, he would stick his head in my office and say, "Do you need anything, Honey? Can I get you a cup of coffee or tea?" Sometimes he even cooked dinner and cleaned the kitchen when I was on a literary roll. He did keep his promise after all: we had the time to do the important things we never did before.

WORDS OF WISDOM: "You are the light of the world...Let your light shine before men, that they may see your good deeds and praise your Father in heaven." Matthew 5: 14, 16

"Never retire. Michelangelo was carving the Rondanini just before he died at eight nine. Verdi finished his opera Falstaff at eighty." W. Gifford-Jones

INSPIRED

☙ ⑥ ❧

A line of poetry promises: "The best is yet to come…" Instead of dreading the loss of youth and vitality, retirement compensates with wisdom, inner strength, and acceptance. Sleepless nights worrying about moving up one more rung on the ladder of success were no longer an occurrence. Self-conscious glances in a mirror to assess our looks were unnecessary because we weren't trying to impress others. No particular bedtime meant Wayne could stay up and finish reading that history book, and I could finish watching *Mr. Smith Goes to Washington* on Turner Classic Movies. I discovered this was a magical time to create each day the way I wanted it to be. The magical part was to *create* which means "call into being."

Retirement was an opportunity for Wayne and me to check off items on our Bucket lists, to add or delete things from our To Do lists that we discovered did or did not matter, and to leave nothing undone that was important for us to complete. Current statistics substantiated that seniors were going back to get college degrees in record numbers, attending seminaries, taking writing classes, writing novels, or life stories as legacies for future generations. Others wanted to play golf, pickle ball, become senior cheerleaders, experience international cuisines, and develop new friendships. There were some retirees who just wanted to sit on the front porch for a while and take long, deep breaths and exhale slowly.

Unfortunately, doctors warn us that a surprisingly high percentage of people die within a few years after retirement. One possible theory for these deaths is that many seniors see retirement as the end of a productive life not the beginning of a new one. Some retirees see no reason to get up in the morning because they have no grand expectations for their lives any longer. Grand expectations might be painting a four board fence to one person or writing a best-selling novel to another, but we all need them. Each heart beats to its own rhythm, but you have to listen to your heart to hear where it is leading you.

My husband's retirement was unlike any of my imaginations. After almost forty years of marriage, I was astonished to discover that I really didn't know as much about Wayne as I thought I did. I knew the part of him that was left over after work. I was accustomed to how he dealt with family issues. I knew what to expect from him in maintaining the nuts and bolts of our everyday existence. Retirement was like peeling off the layers of obligations, responsibilities, and my expectations of my most intimate companion for all these years to ultimately reveal the essence or who he really was at the core of his being.

I needed advice, big time, at the beginning of this journey together because Wayne and I were unsure about what we were going to do with each other now that we were "joined at the hip." Although there were many times throughout the years when I wondered what was I thinking when I decided to marry a person so completely clueless about me; in retirement, I realized I was pretty clueless about him, too. I've learned more about myself and my partner in this retirement journey than all the other years we've been together. God whispered in my ear so loud at times that it was impossible to miss the lesson He wanted me to learn. The boot episode was one of those moments.

In my downsizing phase, I was separating into piles the items I wanted to hang on to, give away to others, or throw away in the trash. I came across a pair of Wayne's most well-worn cowboy boots. My first impression was to toss them in the throw away pile. Then I remembered that I was with him years ago when he bought them. They were shiny black, fine quality leather boots, with pointed toes, decorative white stitching onto the top of the vamp and shaft, on two-inch heels. Now the black leather was dull, the white stitching had turned to gray, and the heels were almost completely worn down with several holes in the soles. I couldn't bring myself to put them in the throw away pile.

I secretly put them in a paper bag and carried them in my car to a local shoe repair shop. I asked the cobbler to put new soles and heels on those old cowboy boots. I could tell by the look on his face that he thought I was throwing good money away by trying to repair boots that had seen their best days. But I didn't believe their best days were over yet. I explained that these were very special boots to my husband, and I wanted to surprise him so he could wear them again.

A few days later the cobbler called and said the boots were ready. I couldn't believe my eyes when I walked into the shoe repair shop, and the cobbler handed me a pair of cowboy boots. Could these be the sad looking pair of boots I dropped off? The black leather was shining again, and the heels and soles gave the boots an *attitude*, at least to me, of "How do you like me now?" When I presented the rejuvenated boots to Wayne, he slipped them on and smiled like he had reconnected with an old friend and went out to work on his six acres. There were definitely going to be good days ahead for those boots.

That boot story illustrates what I've learned about life after I became the wife of a retiree. We start off in life with exciting possibilities and unlimited potential because we are the fearfully and wonderfully made creations of God. Life with all the challenges, family responsibilities, and miles to go before we sleep every day takes its toll on our bodies, and we can't do everything with the vigor we had in our younger days. Then we must choose what to do with our lives in the days we have left on this earth: hang on to the past, give away to others, or throw away in the trash.

I believe, like Wayne's boots, we still have good days ahead travelling with each other on this retirement journey. All we need is the Master Cobbler to cover us with His love and keep us shiny and serviceable, patch the holes in our souls, and send us out to work on our six acres or wherever

He places us in the world. He is the One who gives the Words of Wisdom and provides unfailing advice as we pray and seek His will. He is faithful to every wife when she calls out to Him: **Help! My husband just retired.** I pray that God will grant *calm winds and following seas* to those who are getting ready to disembark at their retirement Port of Call. If you ever find yourself off course, I know where you can find an accurate compass. God is always at the helm.

WORDS OF WISDOM: "Good friend, don't forget all I've taught you; take to heart my commands. They'll help you live a long, long time, a long life lived full and well...Trust God from the bottom of your heart; don't try to figure out everything on your own. Listen for God's voice in everything you do, everywhere you go; he's the one who will keep you on track. Don't assume that you know it all. Run to God! Run from evil! Your body will glow with health, your very bones will vibrate with life! Honor God with everything you own, give him the first and the last." Proverbs 3: 1 – 3, 5 – 12.

****

CPSIA information can be obtained
at www.ICGtesting.com
Printed in the USA
BVHW01s1343291117
501547BV00012B/279/P